# Praise for *Your Invisible Network*

"This is a book that will share immediate practical steps for achieving your career potential. That alone makes it worth the price of purchase. But it's also a fascinating, engaging, entertaining read. Michael Melcher doesn't just know his stuff. He can really write."
—George Stephanopoulos, ABC News, Host of *Good Morning America* and *This Week with George Stephanopoulos*

"We all recognize the value of a network—but how *exactly* do we build our network? In this invaluable resource, Michael Melcher clarifies the process by providing clear strategies, real-life examples and models, and manageable steps. He answers common but thorny questions, such as 'How do I maintain my network as it grows over time?,' 'How do I recognize the signs that someone is willing to help—and how do I handle it if someone ignores me?,' and 'How exactly do I write that email?' *Your Invisible Network* is an instant classic to add to the 'Careers' shelf."
—Gretchen Rubin, Author of *The Happiness Project*, *Better Than Before*, and *The Four Tendencies*, and host of the podcast *Happier with Gretchen Rubin*

"In tech, so many folks are killing it on the hard skills, but cringe and hide under the proverbial desk if you bring up networking. I know—I just hated the idea of having to build a network yet learned the hard way how important it could be. Michael Melcher has written a clear manual with elegant proofs and a sense of humor. *Your Invisible Network* takes the mystery and, most importantly, the stress out of building a personal network in a way that, to quote Michael, 'fits into your life as it is right now.'"
—Daniel Sturman, CTO, Roblox

"Reading *Your Invisible Network* is like getting advice from an expert who also happens to be a close friend. Michael Melcher's relationship-building knowledge is deeply nuanced and global in scale. His words and experience are relevant for professionals in China and India as well as those in the United States."
—Carmen Chang, General Partner and Head of Asia, NEA

"The first thing I noticed about *Your Invisible Network* is that the stories and examples aren't about people described as 'Rob, a regional sales manager.' The book reads like a novel. The stories come alive off the page, perhaps because they are real humans in all their diversity and humanity. And there are plenty of fascinating vignettes about the author himself at different ages, as he learned from trial and error the brilliantly nuanced practices he lays down."
—María Alvarez, Social Impact Leader / Common Sense Latino Founder at Common Sense Media

"The adaptive leaders the world desperately needs in the coming years must have skill and confidence in building and maintaining relationships. Yet this remains an obstacle for many. *Your Invisible Network* demystifies how to take intentional action to expand and improve your relationships. It will be equally relevant to experienced CEOs and to recent grads entering the workforce."
—Pam McLean, PhD, Cofounder & Chief Knowledge Officer, Hudson Institute of Coaching

"Reading this book is like having one of the world's most insightful coaches whispering in your ear. It should be required reading for every soon-to-be graduate and for anyone navigating the inevitable twists and turns of a long and satisfying working life."
—Marci Alboher, VP CoGenerate (formerly Encore.org) and Author of *The Encore Career Handbook* and *One Person/Multiple Careers*

"For both entrepreneurs and investors, relationship building is crucial, yet few have a grasp of how to manage this process. *Your Invisible Network* is the guide we have been waiting for. In clear, compact language, Michael Melcher lays out how to build authentic, reciprocal relationships while you're busy doing everything else, and how to leverage them in ways that are productive and human."
—Soraya Darabi, Cofounder and Managing Partner, TMV

"We all know we need to 'network'—but this is the rare book that gives us very practical and pragmatic advice on how to do that with purpose, and with results that will help in business and in life. We know Michael Melcher's confident yet humble voice from his engagements with PSI, and one of his gifts is to let us learn from his own mistakes and limitations. *Your Invisible Network* reads very differently from most American business books: practical, honest, accessible, and yes, funny. "
—Karl Hofmann, President/CEO, Population Service International (PSI)

"It's been a long time since Michael Melcher was my business school study partner, but I can assure you that his voice is exactly the same: intelligent, warm, funny, and very provocative. What's changed is that he now has several decades of experience seeing exactly what works in building a high-impact career, and in this book he shares it all with you."
—David Sze, Managing Partner, Greylock Partners

"Michael Melcher's genius is his ability to get right to the heart of complicated career issues and provide practical steps to make significant change. He does that in this book. When Michael was my coach during a critical time in my career, I learned that to accomplish something great, competence alone isn't enough. Powerful, reciprocal relationships are crucial. When you finish *Your Invisible Network*, you'll have a plan for reaching your potential—and a dose of Michael's wit along the way."
—Minh-Thu Pham, Cofounder, New American Voices and Lecturer, Princeton University

"For years, Michael Melcher has been a go-to resource for Stanford alumni. One of his skills is breaking down complex, subtle topics into specific, actionable steps. *Your Invisible Network* is a cogent guide to building and managing professional relationships—and also goes a long way to demonstrating how to be a caring, capable human in an imperfect world."
—Carly Janson, Director, Alumni & MSx Career Services, Stanford Business School

"If you are like me, picking up another book on networking is the last thing you want to do. But I loved Michael's book—and you will too—because it's really all about relationships: how to build, nurture, and leverage them so you lead a richer life, and get more of what you seek, professionally and personally. His book is also immensely practical, full of real examples, scripts, and exercises, which reflect what people (and their coaches) truly want and need on this topic. You'll want his book as a handy guide by your side."
—Michael Chang Wenderoth, Executive Coach, Author, *Get Promoted*

# YOUR
# INVISIBLE
# NETWORK

**Also by Michael Urtuzuástegui Melcher**

*The Creative Lawyer: A Practical Guide to Authentic Professional Satisfaction*

*The Student Body* (as Jane Harvard)

# YOUR INVISIBLE NETWORK

## How to Create, Maintain, and Leverage the Relationships That Will Transform Your Career

### Michael Urtuzuástegui Melcher

Matt Holt Books
An Imprint of BenBella Books, Inc.
Dallas, TX

Matt Holt is an imprint of BenBella Books, Inc.
10440 N. Central Expressway
Suite 800
Dallas, TX 75231
benbellabooks.com
Send feedback to feedback@benbellabooks.com

*BenBella* and *Matt Holt* are federally registered trademarks.

Printed in the United States of America
10 9 8 7 6 5 4 3 2 1

Library of Congress Control Number: 2022040500
ISBN 9781637742914 (hardcover)
ISBN 9781637742921 (electronic)

Editing by Gregory Newton Brown
Copyediting by Alyn Wallace
Proofreading by Madeline Grigg and Marissa Wold Uhrina
Indexing by WordCo Indexing Services, Inc.
Text design and composition by PerfecType, Nashville, TN
Author photo by Paul Franz
Cover design by Brigid Pearson
Cover image © Shutterstock / Robert Kneschke
Printed by Lake Book Manufacturing

Special discounts for bulk sales are available. Please contact bulkorders@benbellabooks.com.

*For my beautiful sons, Nico and Mateo*

# CONTENTS

# PART 3: LEVERAGING RELATIONSHIPS

# PART 4: SPECIAL KINDS OF RELATIONSHIPS

# PART 5: KEEPING IT GOING

# INTRODUCTION
## Your Missing Ingredient

Is your career going well? I'm guessing it could go better.

As an executive coach, I've learned what makes people successful—or not. For the past twenty years, I've worked with leaders at the world's top brands, including technology giants, start-ups, law firms, financial institutions, management consulting firms, video game companies, foundations, and nonprofits of all sizes. I've had intimate conversations with stressed-out environmental advocates, plucky company founders, and overworked Wall Street bankers. I've coached people trying to break into particular roles, and coached people who are already in those jobs and trying to do better. I've worked across the United States and in a dozen foreign countries. I've worked with people at all stages of their careers and in every emotional state.

I'm a practitioner, not a theorist. Clients pay me because getting the right results is incredibly important. They don't engage me as a lark. They have big ambitions but limited time and need to know what they can do to improve things. And my clients want more than professional success—they also want a meaningful life with balance and depth.

One of the reasons my profession exists is that there isn't a lot of great advice out there. People invest a lot to prepare for careers. But once their careers are underway, it's less clear what they should do to manage and shape things. You can study engineering at MIT, but there is no MIT for understanding how to build out your network. You could earn a master's degree in foreign relations, but you're not going to find a good master's program in finding mentors and sponsors. If you search online for lessons about professional development, most of the advice you'll find will be strictly bargain bin—a combination of smug platitudes ("It's not what you know, it's who you know"), wishful thinking ("Leap, and the net will appear"), and fear-based recommendations ("Never look for a job without having a job"). There *are* valuable lessons out there—they are just not widely known. There are energizing ideas, research-based truths, and effective practices for how careers work. Furthermore, there are practical actions you can take, right now, to step things up. The most important of these lessons is the power of relationships.

Relationships are the single most important factor in your career success and professional growth. They are not a nice-to-have; they are the ultimate must-have. If you have solid, expansive, extensive relationships, you can achieve your aims; and if you don't, your career will be hobbled.

By relationships, I don't mean lists of contacts on a social media platform. I mean connections that are real, meaningful, vital, and diverse. Not every relationship needs to be close, and not every relationship will easy, but each needs to be an actual connection between human beings with elements of reciprocity, curiosity, and authenticity.

Your commitment to creating, maintaining, and leveraging relationships will determine a variety of outcomes:

- Whether you make full use of your talents and hard work
- Whether you get better jobs and make successful career changes
- Whether you keep growing or hit a ceiling
- Whether you become a leader or person of influence
- Whether you end up successful and fulfilled in your career

Lastly, relationships are a form of wealth that is under your control. You can create this wealth even if you start with nothing. And once you create it, no one can take it away.

▲▼▲

What are you not seeing right now? Who is just beyond your sight line? What is waiting to be discovered?

Everyone has an invisible network: a large collection of people available for your success that you can only partially see at any given moment. Your ability to tap into this invisible network is as important as any other expertise you develop.

Your network has two dimensions of invisibility. The first is horizontal: you don't yet know many of the people in this network because they are beyond your immediate vision. The second dimension is vertical: many of these relationships are underdeveloped—without additional effort you can't access or even perceive the full potential of different people.

Relationship building isn't most people's full-time job. Most people are busy doing the other core parts of their jobs. If you're a software engineer, you code. If you're an equity research analyst, you research equities. If you're a teacher, you teach. But if you focus only on the core deliverables, eventually a gap will appear between *who you are* and *who you could be*.

Most people allow this gap to emerge without realizing it. They don't contemplate who might contribute to their growth; they don't do the work to build relationships; and they don't learn how to ask for what they want. They are lonelier than they need to be, and they get stuck unnecessarily. It's not that they aren't trying to be successful. They just don't understand the specific ways that relationships are so important.

- Relationships provide you with critical knowledge. They let you know about opportunities. They warn you about risks. They inform you about tradeoffs.
- Relationships stimulate your creativity and hone your critical faculties. They show you how to bring out your best. They push you to master challenges.
- Relationships validate who you are, keep you strong, and boost your happiness.

- Relationships help you navigate workplace politics.
- Relationships allow you to help others and contribute to the greater good.
- Relationships support your ability to be a leader.
- Relationships generate other relationships.

This book is your guide to creating, maintaining, and leveraging the relationships that will transform your career.

## Building Relationships Is How You Overcome Obstacles

Many of my clients started out as outsiders. I was one, too. But starting as an outsider doesn't mean you can't figure out a way in.

Consider Juan José García. The son of undocumented immigrants, Juan grew up in the Oak Cliff neighborhood in Dallas, a working-class neighborhood largely ignored by the city after it was the site of John F. Kennedy's assassination. In eighth grade, Juan was awarded a full scholarship to St. Mark's School of Texas, a tony prep school on the other side of town. The new school was tough—it was far more competitive, and he dropped from the top of his class to the bottom third—but it also gave Juan dramatically different perspectives on what was possible in his life. He played football and discovered things in common with the wealthier kids on the team, even though most of them spent weekends at country clubs and he spent weekends mowing lawns with his father to make ends meet at home.

By college and grad school, he had developed an interest in politics and realized the more relationships he had, the better off he would be. He also discovered he liked meeting people and learned a lot from others and their stories. Working in D.C. after grad school, he got to know ambitious political animals of all backgrounds. These folks took networking to a whole different level. He learned that you could have a mutually beneficial relationship with someone without having a lot in common. Coincidentally, he started running into other first-generation strivers whose experiences mirrored his own.

I met him at a professional event in D.C. I was giving career workshops for political appointees who were about to go into the job market. He told me about ultimately running for political office in Texas, and I could tell he had a *something*. I gave him my card, and we connected on social media.

A couple of years later, I was in Austin for work. I was meeting another coach, Shannon, and her husband, and I invited Juan to join us. He drove three hours to meet us. We discovered that residing in the same apartment building as Shannon and her husband was a big political fundraiser they could introduce him to.

Later, going to law school at night while working full time, Juan took part in a formal leadership program aimed at first-generation professionals. When they got to the part about networking and relationships, some of the other students balked. Networking seemed so awkward and fake. How would you ever find the time? Wasn't it enough they were going to be skilled lawyers? In contrast he thought, *What's the big deal?* Those activities had already become part of his DNA.

Juan García is still young, and his story is just getting started. But it's an instructive one for anyone. Building professional relationships is normal. It takes initiative and intention, but it easily can become part of your normal life.

▲▼▲

During my education and early career, I was interested in macro issues—basically, what we should do as a society. I naturally thought in terms of political, social, and economic systems. I wanted to change the world through grand gestures.

But the work I have done most successfully, and where I have had the greatest fulfillment, has been on the micro level: working with individuals and teams, helping them to figure out how to achieve what they want and be who they want to be. Clients work with me because they want to make their lives better *now*.

Many people assume that mastering professional relationships is a "corporate" thing, an upper-class thing, or a "White" thing. That is incorrect thinking. Living in Manhattan, I am surrounded by people who went to selective schools, work for high-brand companies, and make a lot of money. But many of my clients grew up working-class or lower-middle class, are people of color, immigrated to this country, were the first in their family to go to college, or were the first in their family to hit the big time. They started with little, but they've been successful in building relationship wealth. Their hunger is their fuel.

I know what it's like to quietly hold onto the belief that you might really do something great but aren't exactly sure how to get there. I'm familiar with the yearning to get it right and the fear that you might be missing out on something that could be a game changer. I know what it's like to be ambitious but frustrated.

I am most interested in helping people who feel alone and are facing big career questions on their own. I've written this book so that you will be less alone. You can make it happen for yourself, and I'll show you how.

## Twenty Minutes a Day

Going into the professional world with a vague plan to meet people to advance your career is a bit like ambling through Home Depot with an empty cart and no list. Sure, you can pull random industrial cleaners and dimmer switches off the shelves, but what for?

You've probably had the experience of going to a networking event, getting your badge, and then freezing for a moment as you walk into the ballroom entrance wondering, *Why, exactly, am I here?* I've had this very experience, and I'm an extrovert who likes meeting new people. The freeze isn't because I'm afraid. It's because I haven't quite figured out what I'm supposed to be doing.

The way you are going to accomplish your relationship-building goals is through the Twenty-Minutes-a-Day method. This means you will spend twenty minutes a day working "on" your career rather than "in" your career. You will spend this time on concrete actions that will help you create, maintain, and leverage your invisible network. The Twenty-Minutes-a-Day method lets you know where to start and what to do. It also lets you know when you can stop.

Twenty minutes might not seem like much, but it's enough time to do something real. In five years, you'll have taken one thousand separate actions. The consistency of doing a little bit each day makes the difference.

When you finish this book, you'll have a transformed view of your career, be well into the process of building the assets you need, and have confidence that you are on the right track. Your invisible network will be much more visible. You'll be ahead in the game. And once you get started, you'll never go back.

## A Word About Stories and Names

This book is based on my experience, observations, and learning from twenty years of coaching as well as my overall professional and life experience. I use a lot of stories and concrete examples to illustrate points. The stories are real. In some cases, I've used real names, with permission, and in other cases I've created pseudonyms and masked certain identifying details for privacy.

In the exercises and scripts that accompany the various chapters, I use specific names to make them more vivid, because these are intended to be communications that people would use in the real world. The situations are fictional, and other than my own name and those of a few public figures, the names are fictional as well.

Let's get started.

# PART 1
# What Relationships Are and Aren't

# CHAPTER 1
## How the World Really Works

alley Li came to the U.S. as an adult. She was born and raised in China and in 2007 was admitted to a master's program at Stanford. She enjoyed her studies in political science. She felt her own capacities for thinking expand, and she loved writing her thesis about Taiwanese politics—a topic that would have been hard to write about on the mainland (China officially regards Taiwan as a wayward province, not a legitimate actor to be studied for its unique evolution). Halley's passions were politics, ideas, and scholarship. But as graduation approached, she started moving in another direction. Political science was fun to study but had limited prospects as a career. She wanted to be in the world, not a library, and she wanted to earn a good living.

Her ambition reflected her cultural inheritance. The China she grew up in was peaceful and stable, but it had not always been so. In Chinese, there is a word called "luàn" (乱). Luàn means chaos, and nothing is worse than chaos. Before 1976, China had gone through five hundred years of chaos. Halley had grown up in a period of calm and progress, but her extended family had long memories of how difficult life could be and how circumstances could abruptly change. And in her personal life, she had experienced luàn: her beloved father died when she was a teenager. Halley wanted options and independence. She decided to find a career in the financial sector.

Making a switch from political science to finance is hard in the best of times, and Halley was not looking in the best of times. Her job search coincided with a historic recession that in some ways resembled an economic collapse. She also needed an employer that would eventually sponsor her for a work visa.

Her assets couldn't take her far on their own. While she was hard working, intelligent, and personable, so were many other people. She had a master's degree from an elite institution, but it was in the wrong subject. Before that, she'd graduated from a stellar university in Shanghai, but no one in America had heard of it. All her connections were back in China, and they weren't powerful to begin with. Her network in the U.S. was nascent: just the classmates, professors, and administrators she'd met at Stanford. And Halley wasn't a social butterfly or super networker. Compared with other foreign grad students, most of whom studied STEM subjects, she believed she was more outgoing and curious. But when she compared herself to Americans, she felt she lacked confidence and easy camaraderie. Americans had a sense of easy optimism—things would work out!—that she envied.

Basically, Halley was starting from scratch.

One benefit she had was seeing hard truths clearly. Halley was under no illusions that her search would be easy. She knew she would be successful only through a person-by-person approach. This was one advantage of growing up in China: she'd learned not to assume that you could do everything by yourself, that you would just write an application or go to an interview, and be handed a great opportunity. There was *always* a relationship element. Hence while the idea of networking in the United States was intimidating, it was still familiar. She was ready to network, if not for joy, then certainly for survival.

She used her university contacts to get the names of other potential contacts. She landed an appointment with one of the MBA career advisors even though she didn't attend business school. She worked the alumni network, homing in on people who worked and lived in New York. This is how I met her: a career advisor at the business school recommended she reach out.

She wrote a perfect email to me. By "perfect" I mean it was professional; straightforward; specific, yet open; not too long; and respectful, but not needy. We met. I was fascinated by how well she was doing things. She saw herself as someone making zero progress, and I saw someone who was competent, polite, professional, and relentless in doing the work around networking. I asked her how much she needed to earn to survive. "Around nine hundred dollars a month," she answered. *That's nuts!* I thought, but, yes, by living with several roommates in Queens, subsisting on instant noodles, and engaging in no activities other than networking, she kept her expenses low. (Halley later told me that the real number was a thousand, but she didn't want to sound greedy.)

"Let's plan our next appointment," I said. I wanted to help her with her communications, both in networking and interviews. She tried to pay. "Don't be ridiculous!" I answered. A mentorship opportunity showed up out of the blue—for me!—and I grabbed onto it.

Many years later, Halley appeared on my podcast. I had asked her to tally how many people she'd spoken with back then. Long story short, over a ten-year period, she'd had 435 networking meetings. They spanned her initial job search, to her next job search, to trying to get into business school, to making the most of business school, to her jobs afterwards, plus all the ongoing connections she was trying to build to make the most of her various positions.

Most of these conversations were not spectacular. She did not establish deep bonds with most of the people she spoke with. She still felt like a bit of stranger to many people she connected with. But over time, she made major progress. A small percentage of useful meetings adds up. She achieved her evolving goals. She launched a career in finance, moved into new jobs, navigated challenges, and found mentors and sponsors. She married and had children. She was able to create a life for herself—and I emphasize life rather than career.

Halley Li was successful because she somehow grasped many of the best practices and truths about relationships, and she pushed herself to keep learning more. She was willing to do the work. You can read Halley Li's story as an interesting narrative about a particular person. But it also illustrates many of the truths that underlie effective relationship building: She built her network from nothing. She assumed that she could reach out to relative strangers. She built relationships that led to other relationships. She valued people as much for information and feedback as for leads. She met key "weak ties" that were transformative and more useful than people she knew well. She hoped for great connections but wasn't unduly disappointed when things didn't lead anywhere. She shifted her network from one domain to another. She invested a ton of time for a benefit that might not pay off for years. She practiced optimism, openness, and persistence. She viewed herself as the leader of her own life. She was dauntless. She created something that didn't exist before.

▲▼▲

Relationships are crucial for you to reach your potential, but most people are failing at building the professional relationships they need. They are not cultivating their invisible networks as well as they could. They're doing things wrong, or they're not doing them at all. They may have a general idea of what to aim for, but don't take the first step. Or they take the first few steps and then they sort of . . . let go.

In this chapter, I'm going to lay out all the different components of relationship building. Then in each subsequent chapter, we'll dig deeper into how you can master all of them.

## 1. An Overall Strategy

You require a strategy that addresses three key aspects of professional relationships. These are:

- Creating relationships
- Maintaining relationships
- Leveraging relationships

Most people are better at one than the other two. Maybe you're good at keeping in touch with existing friends, but it's harder for you to make new connections. Or maybe you easily meet lots of people but you don't keep up with them—out of sight, out of mind. Leveraging relationships means accessing and asking, and most people feel angst about asking for things. A minority are comfortable with the asking but don't quite get the art of it. They're too pushy or too imprecise.

For your strategy to work, it needs to fit into your life as it is right now. I'm not going to ask you to take on a new job or become a new person. The work we're doing is intended to become part of how you normally operate. You're more likely to change your life if you don't have to change your whole life. Thinking about making big changes can be dramatically interesting but often just keeps you stuck.

## 2. An Understanding of How Relationships Work

You might spend a lot of time analyzing personal relationships—with a spouse or romantic partner, a family member, or a high-maintenance friend. It's less likely you spend time analyzing what is going on in relationships with professional colleagues, clients, or distant acquaintances. Yet these relationships follow an underlying code as much as more intimate ones. Relationships are based on reciprocity, an exchange between two people, and that exchange is based on needs—your needs and the other person's needs. Understanding the elements of relationships and being able to apply them to *all* your relationships, regardless of type, will help you create new relationships and deepen the ones you already have. It will also help you in trickier situations, such as dealing with bosses or more senior people, or in patching things up when a relationship has run into tension.

## 3. A Delineation of the Different Types of Relationships You Need

Once upon a time there was a thing called a Rolodex. It was a small metal office tool that had a cylindrical core, to which you could attach, in alphabetical order, any number of tabbed rectangular cards with the names of your contacts. You'd spin the Rolodex to find the person you needed. You could watch the Rolodex grow thicker and thicker over time as you became more experienced and more impressive. "She has a good Rolodex" was high praise for someone with a good network.

But building a useful network isn't the same thing as having a good Rolodex, or a big one. Having lots of contacts doesn't mean you win. What you want is to have *good* relationships with *specific categories* of people, and then make sure you *maintain those relationships*.

Some of these categories are visible to you—your friends and close colleagues, for instance. Others are less visible—your "weak ties," potential mentors, or possible sponsors that you may not even know yet. Some are people you'd naturally connect with—friends or people from similar backgrounds. Others are people you wouldn't naturally connect with or aren't quite sure how to deal with. One of the themes of this book is that mastering your invisible network isn't about making everyone your friend. You will make lots of good friends, but don't limit yourself to that goal. Familiarity isn't the same thing as usefulness.

In chapter four, I introduce the relationship portfolio. This is the overall collection of people you need to have relationships with, by specific category. I will also provide you with a handy tool—the Relationship Portfolio Bingo Card, a way to track which people you are going to connect with at any given time.

## 4. Practices for Reaching Out

To make the most of your invisible network, you will have to take the initiative. Instead of seeing what comes your way, you're going to reach out. The trouble is, people won't always respond, or respond quickly, or respond in the way you want. You need some practices for dealing with that.

One of the important truths you'll take away from this book is the idea of "the strength of weak ties." This is elaborated on in chapter three and basically means that people you don't know well can have a big positive impact on your career. Part of the work is drawing these weak ties in. But because they are weak ties with whom you don't have an ongoing exchange, you might feel uncomfortable. I will provide scripts for how to reach out and some advice for how to deal with the discomfort.

## 5. Knowing How to Bring Forth the Magical Part of Conversations

Most people don't quite understand how networking conversations work. The greatest benefit from networking conversations is from the unexpected part—what I call "Minute 32"—the ideas and connections that come out after you've gone through your planned agenda. You therefore need some structure to get the conversation going. We will provide guidance for this in chapter seven.

However, you can't predict ahead of time which conversations will be most useful. Some of them will be pretty good, some will seem like a waste of time, and some will be transformational. Therefore, you need to be able to enter conversations without certainty they will lead to particular outcomes.

## 6. A Set of Tools for Deepening Relationships

A connection is the beginning of a potential relationship, but it's not a relationship in itself. Once you reach out and make a connection, you can do specific things to take things further:

- **Following up.** This can include exploring points of commonality, understanding the other person's needs and communicating your own, and finding ways to make the relationship multidimensional—moving from professional to personal, or from virtual to in person.
- **Introducing vulnerability.** Being human isn't just telling the world how great and on top of things you are. It also means sharing your uncertainties, unresolved questions, and fears. This in turn invites the other person to do the same. We will cover how to do this in professional relationships in chapter eight.
- **Recognizing and exchanging "bids."** A bid is an invitation to take a relationship farther. Bids are often buried inside other questions, statements, and actions. Just as important as making bids is recognizing when others are making them and responding appropriately. We review this in chapter two.
- **Dealing with relationship tensions.** Tensions are normal and inevitable. Even though both sides are implicated in any tension, there are actions you can take to resolve them. We cover this in chapter two.

## 7. Persistence

Relationship building requires persistence. You're not going to achieve your maximum if you require immediate gratification. You might achieve some quick wins, but the real benefits come from long-term attention. There are several reasons for this.

First, when you make efforts to intentionally build relationships, you are attempting to disrupt homeostasis—you want something different from what is happening on its own. But other people have their own schedules and priorities.

Second, certain types of relationship building only bear fruit after many years of effort. This often happens in business development or sales roles.

Third, some industries are just harder for building key relationships—not impossible, just harder. These are often industries that are perceived as glamorous, or that pay high salaries, or that are dealing with important public issues. There is a lot of competition, and the skills may be very specialized. Examples are journalism, publishing, television writing, venture capital, private equity, and foundations.

Fourth, relationships become more valuable over time. A colleague you barely know today might be a bridge to a great new job in ten years. People tend to become more successful over time—an aspiring television writer who today is a writers' assistant in fifteen years may be a showrunner or producer. You can be a beneficiary of their success, provided you maintain the relationship.

You need a gut-level willingness to work hard and persevere. We will cover this in chapter twelve.

## 8. A Strategy for Managing a Growing Network

As you grow in work and life experience, you are likely to have more and more relationships. Your "weak tie network" in particular will get bigger and bigger. There is an inherent tradeoff here: the more people in your network, the less time you have to spend with any given person.

Hence, you need practices for managing this growing network so it doesn't become like that out-of-control junk drawer in your kitchen that you fear and love to avoid. This requires you to have a mix of ways of keeping in touch, some of which do not take a lot of time.

You'll benefit if you have a contact management system that works for your personality.

## 9. An Understanding of How to Engage with Mentors and Sponsors

Mentors and sponsors can have a big positive impact on your career. As we will discuss in chapter fourteen, these titles are not as distinctive as you might think: there is a continuum of how people help you (and how you can help people), and people may move along this continuum from stranger to networking contact to mentor to sponsor.

You need to know what you are looking for and also be able to recognize when someone is offering to step up into a new role. This is not always obvious.

## 10. Confidence in Dealing with Bosses and Hierarchy

A robust network includes people more senior to you. They are higher up in the hierarchy, however you define it: older, wiser, more experienced, higher in status, more powerful.

There is nothing unusual about this. It's normal. (You are also more senior to people in your network.) You want a method of engaging with people across hierarchy. As we will discuss, this is more about respect than deference, and avoiding the temptation to "otherize" people above you in the hierarchy. They are people, too, with the same sorts of needs as anyone else.

We will cover this in chapter fifteen.

## 11. Knowing How to Ask

Leveraging relationships is a Goldilocks conundrum: you need to make asks in a way that is not too heavy, not too light, but just right.

To ask for things successfully, you need to know what you are asking for. People fail when they haven't reflected on their own needs, which may change over time. If someone says, "How can I help you?" you should have an answer.

Knowing *how* to ask is complicated because what's most useful and appropriate varies by the situation. When it comes to *what* you're asking, there is a spectrum of general to specific; and when it comes to *how* you're asking, there is spectrum of indirect to direct. Figuring out where to land in the spectrum is an art. But it's one you can learn, and I'll provide scripts that demonstrate how to do it.

## 12. Acting as a Benefactor

Making the most of your invisible network isn't just about investing in "up"—people who can help you. It's also about investing in "down"—people who you can help.

People think they need to attain a certain level of wealth, status, and experience to give back in substantial ways. That's not true. You can give of yourself right now. Further, when you think of yourself as a benefactor— munificent, a philanthropist, a generous eminence—you change the whole energy equation of your career. The more you give, the easier it is to receive.

We'll cover this in chapter sixteen.

## 13. Exercising Your Convening Power

Relationships don't just exist one-on-one. They also exist in groups. A powerful method of leveraging your relationships is developing your own convening power. When you exercise your convening power, you are changing the game altogether. You are shifting from being the person in the relationship to the person who creates the space for multiple relationships to flourish. This takes intentionality and investment of energy over a period of time, but it's very doable, and it benefits you as much as it benefits others. We will cover how to exercise your convening power in chapter thirteen.

## 14. Confidence and Tools for Setting Boundaries

You're not the only person who will ask people for things. Other people will ask you for things, too. The more senior you get, the more you are going to receive requests from people you could help. This will be accentuated if you are the first in your community to make it somewhere. You will be seen as both powerful and familiar, and the combination means you will be the target of lots of asking.

The question is who you choose to help. Creating a general reciprocal flow between you and the world doesn't mean that you comply with every request you get.

In chapter seventeen, I will introduce some frameworks that help you decide what you are going to do and for whom. This will help you set boundaries that are right for you.

Those are the core components. I'm going to explain these topics in depth in the subsequent chapters and show you how to achieve mastery, step by step. But because the purpose of providing all these ideas and practices is to benefit you and your career, let's start with a check-in on where you are in your career and relationship development.

### Exercise 1: Career and Relationship Audit

Let's start by getting a quick, clear sense of how your career and relationships are going.

1.  What are your current career and personal goals?
2.  What's going well in your career?
3.  What's going less well?
4.  How do you hold yourself back?
5.  How do others hold you back?
6.  Where do you see yourself in one year? In five years? In ten years?
7.  What is a positive change you would like to see in yourself?

## Exercise 2: Relationship Role Models

Think of someone who is good at building relationships—someone you admire. This might be someone you know or someone out in the world.

1. Who is this person?
2. Why do you admire them?
3. What do they do that makes them effective at building relationships?
4. What's an attribute of this person that you share?
5. What's an attribute that seems more distant for you, but that you would like to develop?

## TWENTY-MINUTES-A-DAY EXERCISES

- **Exercise 1:** Review the list of fourteen activities in this chapter's list of components of relationship building. Identify three that you want to focus on. Write these on a Post-it, and put that note in a place where you'll see it regularly, as a visual cue.
- **Exercise 2:** Review the fourteen components of relationship building again; for each of these, jot down the name of someone who seems particularly skilled in that area.
- **Exercise 3:** Pick one of the people you've listed. Send them an email and say, "I'd like to catch up. Can I get some time on your calendar?" Plan to ask how they approach the skill or area of understanding identified in your list.

# CHAPTER 2
# The Relationship Code

One of the most important relationships in my life has been with Caitlin, the woman who agreed to be our surrogate and carried my twins. Caitlin has no biological connection to my children—an egg donor and I formed an embryo, and this was placed in Caitlin's uterus—but she has immeasurable, unequalled importance in our lives.

Surrogacy is a legally and emotionally complex process, and expensive as all get out. There are no guarantees of any kind. But the kind of people who do surrogacy—mainly gay men and heterosexual couples who face fertility issues or complications in giving birth—have long since figured out that no one guarantees you the ability to be a parent.

Matching with your surrogate is a huge step forward in the process. It can take a long time, but in our case it was easy. Caitlin was the first potential surrogate I met, and I was the first intended parent she met.

While Caitlin and I felt an immediate trust—we picked each other after a single phone call—I found it difficult to connect in other ways. I was from New York, and she was from a small town in rural Minnesota. I was a lapsed Catholic and she was a religious Protestant. I was a childless gay guy trying to become a dad, and she had married her high school sweetheart at eighteen. I wrote a three-page essay that featured pictures of my partner and me holding three Sheltie puppies, and she wrote a two-paragraph essay that featured a picture of her with her husband and kids, all wearing football uniforms. We did have something in common: my family thought I was doing something weird, and her family thought she was doing something weird as well.

I feel confident talking to most people. I take it as a challenge to figure out a connection. But my phone calls with Caitlin felt stilted, and my emails and texts did not do much better. When I visited her for the first time, before the embryo transfer, I met her entire extended family in a Pizza Ranch in Luverne, Minnesota. There were twenty or so people there who had showed up to support her, yet I found it hard to spark conversation, with the exception of a long talk I had with her sister-in-law about the Myers-Briggs Type Indicator.

Caitlin got pregnant easily, and we had a few calm weeks. Then, at the first ultrasound, the technicians heard two heartbeats. Not one. Two. The single embryo we transferred had divided. I was stunned, as was she. I thought (wished?) that perhaps the ultrasound equipment in her small town wasn't up to par and the reading was mistaken. No dice. The stakes rose suddenly because when you discover you are having twins, you immediately fall into the category of "high-risk" pregnancy. There is a much higher chance of early birth and double the chance of birth defects, many of which you cannot detect until twenty weeks. Identical twins have higher risks than fraternal twins.

A twins pregnancy was as much a shock to Caitlin as it was to me. Part of the matching process in surrogacy is to ensure that you are aligned in terms of important medical and life decisions: how much of a relationship you will have after the baby is born, whether you will use amniocentesis, under what circumstances you will terminate, whether you will transfer more than one embryo. We had agreed: just one embryo! Caitlin knew *a lot* about pregnancy. She had delivered three healthy children. She knew that twins would be a whole different ball game. The day after the ultrasound, we were transferred to the big teaching hospital in Sioux Falls, forty-five miles from her hometown.

Our nascent relationship was challenged big time. We also learned more about each other. "You ask a lot of questions," she said, after our first ultrasound appointment with the specialist in Sioux Falls. I'd attended by phone. "You ask more questions than anyone I've ever met." It did not sound like a compliment. She wasn't wrong. Not only do I ask a lot of questions, but I feel it's required of me to ask questions. My understanding of life is that if I don't ask the right questions, then it's my fault if things go wrong. Caitlin's life was less based on asking every potential question. It was more about doing your duty, following your principles, and respecting authority.

In this uncertain, scary period, communication was not about entertaining each other or discovering cool similarities. It wasn't about chatting each other up and learning about each other's families. Our communication focused on the development of two fetuses, as well as Caitlin's own health. She had to take multiple drugs for this process to work, and they had side effects. Every two weeks was another ultrasound appointment. As each one approached, the adrenaline in my body rose precipitously, and after each successful appointment, I'd be overcome with wild joy.

Something else was growing—our relationship, which had its own life independent of anything else. There was no dramatic before or after point, but I clearly remember one day in the fall, around fourteen weeks into the pregnancy. I'd flown to Minnesota to attend one of the appointments. My eighty-two-year-old mother met me there to show support. I drove to see Caitlin, and we went to Pizza Ranch with her three kids.

Caitlin looked stressed and down. Taking one look, my mom said she would look after the kids to give us some time. I asked Caitlin how she was feeling. I already knew the pregnancy had been much harder than her prior three. The combination of twins and weird fertility drugs took a toll. Her husband had been consistently and unrestrainedly supportive, but she was physically very uncomfortable. She felt that a lot of people in her small town were judging her. She also felt scared, although probably less than I did.

"I'm sorry you're feeling so bad. It sounds bad. That sucks. You do look really uncomfortable. I'm sorry about that. How are you dealing with everything?" I said variations of those things while I silently told myself, *Don't try to solve her problem, don't try to solve her problem. Just be with her.*

We drank soda and ate some pizza, and we sat together for a while. Then we gathered up the kids and left. A local woman made a mildly judgy comment about one of her kids, and Caitlin and I shared an eye roll. Nothing really happened that day, but something did become clear, at least to me: *We were in it.* Together.

The closer we got to a normal delivery date, the better we felt. Each ultrasound went well. "Perfect as always," the specialist OB-GYN said.

"I think it's because of me," Caitlin said. "I'm good at baking babies."

I nodded my agreement. "You have excellent core competencies for being pregnant."

Nicolás and Mateo were born early, but not incredibly early: thirty-five-and-a-half weeks, which is pretty good for twins. They were healthy, gorgeous, and perfect in every way. They weighed around six pounds each. "Your babies are adorable," the nurses told me, and they decorated the NICU room with construction paper cutouts of their names. The babies spent eleven days in the NICU, and Caitlin spent a lot of time with them, as did her children, her husband, her parents, her mother-in-law, her siblings, and a few other people. I learned how to feed my sons, how to change them, and how to swaddle them. I practiced skin-to-skin contact while watching old episodes of *RuPaul's Drag Race* and *Hell's Kitchen* on my iPad. I wondered how to thank Caitlin, beyond what I'd done already, so I asked my friends on Facebook to share their appreciation on my behalf. Two hundred people from around the world chimed in, including a lot of mothers who had twins or who had experienced fertility issues.

Our family's relationship with Caitlin and her family has continued, not because it had to, but because it just did. I went to Minnesota a total of six times, and she and her husband have visited us several times.

Nothing is uncomfortable now. I feel I could talk to her about almost anything. Neither of us has changed. We are the still the same people who did our best in the awkward matchmaking call eight-plus years ago. What has changed is that we developed a real relationship by experiencing one of life's most powerful experiences. Our relationship deepened not because of my clever tricks, but in spite of them.

## What Makes Relationships Work?

Relationships are bridges that connect you to knowledge, opportunities, and people. But the thing is, a bridge is an actual something. It must have some real substance, not be ephemera. If you don't understand what relationships are and how they work, they stay invisible.

The "relationship code" that I will describe will help you clearly see the engineering inside any relationship. You will go beyond winging it to knowing how to apply clear principles for how relationships develop. You can use this code to diagnose what might be missing from relationships that haven't taken off or those that have fallen off course.

## Six Rules of Relationships

The relationship code consists of six rules:

1. Relationships are connections between two people with a reciprocal beneficial exchange. However, reciprocity is rarely exact.
2. Relationships are the negotiation of needs—your needs and my needs. The relationship is the intersection of these.
3. Relationships start and grow through "bids." A bid is a specific effort to take the relationship further.

4. Relationships deepen through transparency and curiosity. This involves vulnerability, which is necessary but poses risk—you don't know how the other person will respond to what you are sharing or asking. You can develop the habit of taking what author David Bradford and Carol Robin call "15 percent risks."

5. Relationships can be built with people quite different from you. You need flexibility to adapt to difference, but the underlying code is the same.

6. Relationship problems are often caused by a breakdown or change in the "your needs, my needs" equation.

Like most principles about living, these sound straightforward. It is in the application that we will see their power.

## 1. Reciprocal Exchange

A relationship is a connection between two people with a reciprocal beneficial exchange. Exchange includes giving, receiving, and sharing. You can give, receive, and share many things:

| 1. Experiences | • You were in Marines bootcamp together<br>• Your surrogate, egg donor, and you partnered to make a child<br>• You were next-door neighbors for ten years |
|---|---|
| 2. Similarities | • You are both rapier wits and entertain each other in conversation<br>• You and your friend both went to HBCUs and are now working in finance<br>• You both love talking about reality television |

| 3. Information, Advice, Feedback | • You provide advice to a rural high school student on how to think about college<br>• You tell your friend how to get a job as a congressional staffer<br>• You recommend a book to your cousin that you think he will like |
| --- | --- |
| 4. Interest, Attention, Concern | • You show an interest in someone's kids<br>• You ask about someone's childhood in the Great Depression<br>• You call to check in on your friend who moved back to San Antonio |
| 5. Gifts and Celebration | • You attend your roommate's citizenship ceremony<br>• You pay for your niece's sports fees<br>• You organize people to make a birthday video for a friend |
| 6. Presence and Time | • You visit your voice teacher when she's in the hospital<br>• You pull your roommate's hair back when she is throwing up<br>• You have coffee or a drink with a friend just to catch up |
| 7. Help, Service, Contribution | • Your colleague introduces you to her financial planner<br>• You visit a mom with a newborn and tidy up their kitchen<br>• You do practice interviews with your friend before her big interview |
| 8. Appreciation, Validation, Respect | • You send your former boss an email saying how much you learned from him<br>• You take notes when your mentor talks, and ask thoughtful questions<br>• You arrange for the second graders to send thank-you notes to the firefighter who came to speak to the class |
| 9. Interventions, Sponsorship, Use of Political Capital | • You write a recommendation for a former student and follow it up with a call<br>• You ask the new hire about her career interests<br>• You draft a letter that your cleaning lady can use to ask the college for more financial aid for her daughter |

Relationships can grow out of many different foundations. With Caitlin, I assumed we should start with shared similarity (the second category in the table above) and searched for something that we would connect on. I tried gifts and showing interest, sending bagels to her family and mailing Halloween cards to each of her kids (categories four and five). But ultimately our relationship was rooted in the experience we shared (category one). We were in it together, we relied on one another, and no one else had the perspective we did. And *that* created something lasting.

In professional relationships, the reciprocity is often inexact. Someone could offer you insightful career advice, and you may offer that person appreciation. That is okay.

Reciprocity can also be asynchronous: you could do an important favor for someone today, and it might be five years later that they do something for you. You usually cannot predict how you might help someone in the future. It's one of the beautiful things about relationships—time will pass and then suddenly your interests merge in a new way.

## 2. My Needs, Your Needs

I have my needs, you have your needs, and our relationship is the negotiation of those needs.

There's often a difference between a position—what you say you want—and the need underneath. Everyone has needs, and the more you can identify the other person's actual needs, the better you can manage the relationship. Further, the more curious you are about your own needs, the more clearminded you are going to be when it comes to relationships. When people argue for a long time or coexist in mutual frustration, it's often because they're locking into positions that do not reflect their underlying needs instead of attending to them.

Sometimes needs are obvious, and sometimes they require some digging. Particular positions can represent different needs. As you read the entries in the following table, first read the statement on the left and ask, "Why is this important to that person?" Then read potential needs on the right.

| Position | Need |
|---|---|
| • I want to see this movie. | • I need entertainment.<br>• I need time where it's just us together. |
| • You're leaving me out of the loop. | • I need to feel included.<br>• I need information necessary to do my job. |
| • I don't want to go to Paris; I want to go to Florida. | • I need sun.<br>• I need relaxation. |
| • I don't want to go to Florida; I want to go to Paris. | • I need stimulation.<br>• I need discovery. |
| • I don't want to start our meetings with lengthy personal check-ins. | • I need to use my limited time effectively.<br>• I need to resolve the issues in front of us. |
| • I want to start meetings with a personal check-in. | • I need to feel connected to everyone.<br>• I need to express what I'm experiencing before I can dig into business. |
| • You never give me positive feedback. | • I need to feel valued.<br>• I need to feel I am growing. |

## 3. Making, Recognizing, and Answering Bids

A few years ago, I took a swimming improvement class at the local YMCA in western Massachusetts, where we spent a few years while my kids were in preschool. The class was titled "Masters Swimming" (indicating an advanced skill in the sport), and while for me the title was extremely aspirational, our instructor, Harrison Ross, took the class very seriously. Twice a week he'd create a series of lessons and drills for the four of us in the class, and throughout the hour he would pace along the length of the pool examining our performance. A recent college grad, he was less than half the age of his students, but his youthful brain housed an expert ability to analyze the countless factors involved in swimming correctly and well.

While I am a dutiful student in any class, I took advantage of any breaks between drills to chat with the other students and our instructor and, basically, not swim for a minute or two. In response to a comment Harrison made about wanting to read more, I told him about Cal Newport's book, *Deep Work*, and gave him a quick synopsis. (Synopsis: minimize distractions when you work because they are degrading your brain power and you are capable of far more.)

The following week, after our workout, Harrison said, "I looked up that book you mentioned and started reading it. It's really interesting. I'm starting to use some of the author's tips." This was noteworthy. Most people don't follow up on suggestions of books to read, even if they write down the title and author.

Then he said, "I also looked you up. I checked your website and some things you've written. You have a really interesting career. I'd love to learn more about coaching and how you got started. It's something I've been thinking about." This was also unusual. Some people look me up online, but it's rarer when someone I meet in real life takes this step.

Over the next few months, Harrison and I got together a couple of times. I listened to him and gave him some suggestions for resources. He later moved to Boston and we met a couple of times there.

Shortly after the pandemic started, he sent me an email out of the blue. He had time on his hands and wondered whether there was any work he could do for me. He volunteered to be an unpaid intern for anything I might think of, writing, "You are always up to interesting things, and I think I could learn a lot from you."

As it happened, I had been thinking of launching a podcast about careers (what eventually became *Career Stewardship with Michael Melcher*). I was also contemplating the early form of this book, although the specific shape wasn't entirely clear to me.

Harrison did become my intern, and he was fantastic. He was able to help in all sorts of ways that I wouldn't have anticipated, such as handling a lot of the tech stuff related to podcasting and sourcing someone to design a logo. And during this process we talked a lot about his own plans, ambitions, and questions. Our relationship continues—a friendship from my point of view, and most likely a mentorship from his point of view.

This relationship came about because both of us, but particularly Harrison, recognized how to make and respond to bids.

Bids are how relationships deepen. A "bid" is a statement, request, or action that signifies that you are interested in moving forward.

Say someone says to you: "I'm thinking of taking this course on Web 3. Do you want to take it with me?"

This request potentially has two meanings. The first is the simple question of whether you are interested in the course. The second is a relationship bid. Consider these possible underlying meanings:

- "I would like us to have this fun experience together."
- "Let's get to know each other outside of work."
- "I'd like your advice on what I should be learning."

Bids occur at the start of relationships and continue all the way through them. Here are some examples of what bids can sound like:

- "Let's grab lunch sometime."
- "I'd like to add you to my LinkedIn network."
- "I thought you might find this TED Talk interesting, so I'm sending it along."

- "Mateo has requested a playdate with Ricky. Is he available this week?" (This is a bid for kid socializing, but it's also a bid for parent socializing.)
- "A group of us are getting together for a drink before the board meeting. Do you want to come?"
- "We have an extra ticket for the Met. Are you free on Friday?
- "I got the book you recommended, and I also looked you up online."
- "I have some extra time. Do you have any projects I might help with?"

Sometimes a bid comes in the form of a request for service:

- "I'm chair of the auction committee. Would you consider joining the committee?"
- "Could you look at this email I'm sending and see if the tone is right?"
- "I need to figure out what to put on my baby registry. Can I come over to your place and have you just tell me what I should get?"

You can accept bids, and you can also raise them. If someone holds a fundraiser and you attend, you are accepting the bid. If you bring two friends or forward the invitation to ten other people, you are raising the bid. If someone invites you to coffee and you say yes, you are accepting the bid. If you then invite them to Thanksgiving dinner, you are raising the bid.

Make bids, and learn to recognize and respond to them.

## 4. Relationships Deepen Through Curiosity and Transparency

In relationships, you talk. *How* you talk can determine whether the relationship stays superficial or deepens. (There are other ways that relationships deepen, such as sharing experiences, but talking is a big one.) Talking in a way that deepens relationships requires curiosity and transparency.

Curiosity means authentic curiosity about another person. As I wrote in my earlier book, *The Creative Lawyer,* if you spend time with someone but they never ask you about your background, experiences, hobbies, opinions, or needs, you probably won't feel close. You feel unseen and may wonder if the person has any actual interest in you.

Transparency means you share more of who you are, including your goals, skills, and ambitions. This can include the parts that aren't so shiny and put together: your fears, doubts, insecurities, and uncertainties.

Good relationships have a balance of these two factors. Keep in mind that the right balance depends on the two specific people involved. Some people go deep quickly, and other people practice more moderation.

One reason work relationships can feel so unsatisfying is that they often lack this combination of curiosity and transparency. It's not uncommon for a person to spend hundreds of hours working with others on a project, but never feel understood as a human. You can be commended for good work and yet feel like shouting, "Hello, there's a person here!"

When I design team leadership programs, I often start with a structured, getting to know each other sequence of activities. Before we do these exercises, many participants predict they will be a waste of time. (*Can't we just get to the substance?*) But these activities *always* work. People are astounded to learn basic things about colleagues they've worked with for years: what makes their day, what their families are like, their special interests, their childhood talents, important or difficult events in their past, you name it. After a team has gone through a few of these conversations, you can feel the shift in the room. It's warmer, more open, more relaxed. Team members have stopped being work robots and started being people who are in relationship with each other.

Working in a company or organization or going to a professional event is different from hanging out with friends. We're at work to do a job. To some degree, we are all managing how people perceive us, which is fine. However,

I will make the case that generally we could be more curious about others, and we could reveal more about ourselves—in other words, we could introduce more vulnerability into relationships. We will examine *how* we do this, including the concept of "15 percent risks," in chapter eight.

## 5. You Can Build Relationships with People Quite Different from You

Don't over-rely on connections that come easily. You can build relationships with people quite different from you, and, what's more, you should.

Early in my coaching career, I tended to interpret the vibe I felt in a session as a sign of whether the client was getting good results. If we had an easy rapport, if they opened up easily, if we hugged at the end of a session, I felt we'd really accomplished something. As for the clients who were more restrained, more skeptical, or who just seemed kind of cold, I thought, well, I'm not going to be everyone's cup of tea.

With more experience, I realized I was misreading things. How people expressed themselves, and whether their self-expression matched my own, were not accurate measures of client progress. People are different. Just because someone didn't hug me didn't mean that he didn't value our sessions, and just because someone did hug me didn't mean that I was amazing.

There are many types of difference and diversity in our world. People have different personalities and different lived experiences. You're poorer than some people and richer than others. Your sex, sexual orientation, ethnicity, and class background may affect how you see the world and possibly how you communicate. They also affect the assumptions you make about others and the assumptions they make about you.

There's nothing wrong with striking quick rapport. It's fun when it happens. But immediate similarity isn't a good screen for determining where you should concentrate your relationship-building efforts. With curiosity, flexibility, and a willingness to learn, you can engage with people across difference. The underlying relationship code is the same.

### 6. Relationship Problems Are Often Caused by a Breakdown or Change in the "Your Needs, My Needs" Equation

Relationships inevitably run into uncertainties, tensions, and problems. You can't solve every relationship problem (particularly since another person is always involved), but in many cases you can improve things by reexamining the "your needs, my needs" equation. Often there has been a change, slippage, or breakdown in that equation. One or both parties' needs are not being met. Figure out what is happening on that deeper level, and then you can act.

The Pinch-Crunch Model (originally called the Pinch Model) is helpful for seeing how breakdowns occur. This model derives from the ideas of John J. Sherwood and John C. Glidewell in the early 1970s.

A crunch is something major. One or both of you are really annoyed. The crunch occupies a lot of space in your brain. When conflict does erupt, both sides already have a stockpile of attributions, are sure of their judgment, and are probably emotional. Constructive conversations are possible, but they take a lot more effort.

In contrast, a "pinch" is a minor irritation, annoyance, or disappointment triggered when your expectations in the relationship have not been met:

- "I worked all weekend on the brief and sent it to the partner, and all he wrote back was, 'Thx.'" (I had the expectation that partner would recognize my dedication and excellent work.)
- "I'm surprised you sent the deck to the client without making sure that the font sizes were consistent on all the slides." (I had the expectation that you would show attention to detail and display professional standards.)
- "When my grown son calls, we'll be having a good conversation and then he just says, 'Okay, gotta go, bye.'"(I had the expectation that my son would be interested in talking with me.)

The pinches may reflect a breakdown in agreed-upon expectations or expectations that you haven't communicated. These expectations are in turn reflections of underlying needs:

1. **My expectation:** That the partner would recognize my dedication and excellent work
   **My need:** Recognition and appreciation
2. **My expectation:** That you would show attention to detail and display professional standards
   **My need:** To depend on you
3. **My expectation:** That my son would be interested in talking with me
   **My need:** To feel loved and relevant

You will notice that the pinches in the examples are not extreme—you're miffed but not debilitated. Nor are they clear-cut cases of wrongdoing. There might be another side to each story. Was the partner being a jerk or just moving through email quickly? Is your direct report not client-ready, or does she not share your concerns about font consistency? Does your son take you for granted, or does he end all his calls this way?

Pinches annoy us, sort of, but we don't want to make a big deal about something small. The problem is that pinches add up. That's because *ignoring* a pinch rarely means *forgetting* it. Instead, we add it to the file, and if we don't discuss it with the other person, we stamp it with our own interpretation. Living with pinches can lead to unconstructive behavior. You might start to bond with others on the basis of shared irritation or antipathy. Research has shown that people bond more quickly on the basis of shared dislikes than shared likes.[1]

---

1. Markham Heid, "How Shared Hatred Helps You Make Friends," Forge, September 6, 2019, https://forge.medium.com/how-shared-hatred-helps-you-make-friends-40f5c988c76a.

The best way to deal with crunches is to prevent them—deal with pinches before they become crunches.

First, return to the "your needs, my needs" equation. David Bradford and Carole Robin, authors of *Connect: Building Exceptional Relationships with Family, Friends, and Colleagues*, advise starting with curiosity. Ask yourself, "I wonder why this isn't working."

Then analyze needs. Go from the dance floor to the balcony, take a look, and ask, "What does each of these people need?" Don't stack the deck by defining your needs as noble ("I just want respect") and the other person's needs as unreasonable ("He's a control freak"). Use reasonable language to describe each side's needs.

Then have some courage and be willing to bring up, *in a calm, respectful way*, something that you might normally ignore. The formula is:

1. This is what happened . . .
2. This is how I felt . . .
3. The story I'm making up in my head is . . .
4. I wanted to check this out with you. What are your thoughts?

Navigating pinches is a way to get better at the hard parts of relationships. They are bite-sized. They have less emotional content. The other person might wonder why you are bringing up something trivial, but they are also more likely to engage since the matter is easier to resolve.

▲▼▲

These are the six rules of the relationship code. Now that you've heard them articulated, you are going to start seeing them in the world, the same way that you see a particular model of car everywhere once you decide to buy it. It will be less of a mystery why relationships work the way they do and what you can do to create the ones you want.

## TWENTY-MINUTES-A-DAY EXERCISES

- **Exercise 1: Understanding the needs of colleagues.** Pick a colleague and answer the following questions:

  1. Who is the colleague? How would you currently assess the health of this relationship?
  2. What are their professional needs?
  3. What are their personal needs?
  4. How confident am I that I know what their needs actually are?
  5. What's a way I currently meet their needs?
  6. What's something else I could do that might support one of their personal or professional needs?

  Example Answers:

  1. Who is the colleague? How would you currently assess the health of this relationship?
     *My colleague, Evelyn. It's a very positive relationship. We work together a lot and trust each other. On the other hand, I'm not very deliberate, and we sometimes have misfires. I give it an 8 out of 10.*
  2. What are their professional needs?
     *Maximize income, have significant role on projects, be allowed to run with it, be respected for her talents and experience.*
  3. What are their personal needs?
     *Explore life, have friends, be around optimistic people who have joie de vivre.*
  4. How confident am I that I know what their needs actually are?
     *These are guesses. I don't think I'm wrong, but there may be something else.*
  5. What's a way I currently meet their needs?
     *Bring her into my projects, give her new client leads, attend her parties.*

6. What's something else I could do that might support one of their personal or professional needs?

*Host a party in my home and ask her to bring five people.*

- **Exercise 2: Trying out other love languages.** The five love languages, conceived by Gary Chapman, are words of affirmation, physical touch, acts of service, quality time, and receiving gifts. (In workplaces, where touching is frowned upon or prohibited, I would substitute "physical proximity" for physical touch.)

1. Assess your own love languages.
2. Think of someone specific. Brainstorm how you could express each of the love languages to that person.

Example Answers:

1. Assess your own love languages.

*My love languages are definitely words of affirmation and physical touch. Gifts are a stretch for me—I have never been into them.*

2. Think of someone specific. Brainstorm how you could express each of the love languages to that person.

*I'll pick Joel, a client I have known for a long time. We have very different politics but get along well.* Words of affirmation: *I could tell him how impressed I am with how he's handled the growth of his firm.* Physical proximity: *I can arrange lunch with him near his office.* Acts of service: *I would need to ask him what I can do to help. Possibly refer candidates to his firm—they are in high-growth mode.* Quality time: *I think lunch counts here as well.* Receiving gifts: *I'll bring him some printed photos of my kids. He loves watching them grow up on Facebook, and I think he would appreciate the gesture.*

- **Exercise 3: Getting honest about pinches.** Think of a relationship in your life where you're aware of some discomfort. You might like the person and value them a lot, but occasionally they get on your nerves or don't do what you want. Fill in the following prompts—you can modify the language of each prompt or skip any that don't apply:

1. Recently, I've found myself mildly irritated at _____ because they _____.

2. For a while, I have had a concern that this person lacks _____.

3. I hesitate to bring things up with this person because they are likely to _____.

4. To be honest, I've talked to a third party about this person. I told the third party that this person was _____. What I should really tell the person directly is _____.

5. An underlying need of mine that is not entirely met in this relationship is _____.

6. An underlying need of this person that is probably not being met in our relationship is _____.

Now plan to have a conversation with this person. You can use the step-by-step method described in this chapter, or you can have a broader "your needs, my needs" discussion.

# CHAPTER 3
## The Science of Strangers

A few years ago, I was in Washington, D.C., when a former business school classmate of mine, Leticia Miranda, invited me to brunch. Leticia and I had known each other in many incarnations—classmates, business partners in a doomed start-up, and members of a circle of friends from business school. We had both been raised by Mexican-American single mothers, and we respected each other as Empowered Chicanos, a term she coined. But it had been a few years since we'd connected.

Leticia thought I might like to meet some friends of her roommate, Soledad Roybal, who worked at the State Department. I felt myself resisting as she made the invitation. I had been in the Foreign Service in my early twenties but had left twenty-five years earlier, and I wasn't sure I wanted to talk with young diplomats about their amazing careers. She said they were diverse and cool, but I questioned the point of meeting people I'd never see again. Also, I have this thing about brunch: I don't like it. It seems *lazy*. And I'm sure I was on some weird diet and was afraid of the carbs. The last thing I wanted was to battle waffles.

But I do try to stretch myself from time to time, and I recognized that Leticia had an excellent track record of introducing me to good people. She is what Malcolm Gladwell would call a "connector."[1] She knows many different types of people and is always enthusiastic about introducing them to each other.

Once I managed to show up and chill out, the brunch was super fun. It was a combination of various State Department people, both career officers and young political appointees—people who had worked on the Obama campaign and then found positions through connections and networking. They were all ethnic minorities, which was an interesting development in the Foreign Service. At least one was gay. (When I was in the Foreign Service, gay people had an ambivalent position at best and were occasionally driven out by the security clearance teams.) The whole group were very interested in coaching and seemed to think I was a pretty cool guy.

Soledad herself was particularly interested and showed some real get-up-and-go. She explained she was trying to bring more professional development opportunities to the appointee group. I hung out at the brunch for several hours.

I followed up after the brunch but didn't see results right away. There were fits and starts: I had a few meetings with Soledad that were pleasant but didn't yield anything. I wrote a proposal or two that didn't go anywhere. But the new relationship with Soledad led to much, much more over the next several years.

It started with a workshop for State Department appointees at Camp David, the famed presidential retreat. Soledad then introduced me to the executive team of Latinos44, a Latino political appointees affiliation group; she was one of the cofounders of the group. They were planning a big conference.

---

1. In *The Tipping Point*, Gladwell identifies three types of people who have disproportionate influence in networks. These are "connectors"—people who know everyone, "mavens"—people who have specific recommendations that you trust, and "persuaders"—people who get you to do things.

I gave them tips on how to engineer the two days for maximum impact and accepted their invitation to lead the keynote workshop, where I totally killed it. After that, I was picked up by Black44 and LGBT44 for similar events and did a bunch of workshops for the White House Personnel office.

In all, I did a dozen pro bono workshops. By pro bono, I mean free, but honestly, I would have paid for this type of opportunity. I love politics, I love helping people figure out their paths, and I love being a big star. I simultaneously felt like a grown-up doing responsible grown-up things, and a kid taking it all in—the East Wing! Camp David! Washington! Also, as a Hispanic person who does not have a Hispanic last name, it felt super validating to be welcomed by this community, not just as a member, but as someone who could do some real good.

Then I got to attend the Democratic National Convention, a dream I'd had since childhood after watching Texas Congresswoman Barbara Jordan give an impassioned address on television at the 1976 convention.

And then I got an invitation to the White House Christmas party, to which I brought my mom. To top off the platters of exquisite food, gorgeous decorations, and military men in braid, multiple people came up to my mom to say how great I was. She luxuriated in the praise.

## What We Know About How People Connect

Let's freeze the video on this story at the point where things started: with an invitation from a friend I hadn't spoken to for a couple of years to a brunch I didn't want to go to. I talked myself out of my reluctance and took an action that promised no special payoff.

I wasn't the only one taking action by attending. So did Leticia. So did Soledad. So did everyone else who participated in that brunch and in every other event in the sequence, individuals who were in many cases connecting with people they didn't know well or at all.

There is science behind what happened at that brunch, and afterwards. In this chapter, I'm going to outline what we really know about how networks function as they pertain to your career. Specifically, we're going to analyze the science of strangers: how we go from individuals who don't know each other to people who can help one another, and why accessing these relationships is critical for your career progress.

There are six truths about how networks function and how to get the optimal benefits from them:

1. Merit is necessary but not sufficient.
2. The business world is more democratic than you think.
3. How you say things matters.
4. Networks become more valuable over time.
5. You must harness the strength of weak ties.
6. Make social contagion work for you.

## Truth #1: Merit Is Necessary but Not Sufficient

Merit-based systems are good. It makes moral and economic sense that people should advance according to merit. However, this is not how things work. Merit is required, but it's not enough. This can be a hard pill to swallow.

A colleague and I conducted several career workshops at the Hong Kong University of Science and Technology over a three-day period. A third of the student population was from Hong Kong, a third from China, and a third from everywhere else. On Friday night we started with our networking workshop, which had been a consistent crowd pleaser. But the evaluations we distributed after the session told a different story this time: the students hated the workshop! Chastened, we continued for the rest of the weekend, trying to figure out what was going on. Gradually things turned around, and by the end they liked us.

Here's what I determined: students were coming to this MBA program because they wanted to improve their careers. They'd invested a lot of time and money in a degree program that promised that. And then we showed up and said, "Oh, by the way, you need to network the hell out of things to be successful." Their reaction was anger, because that's how you might respond when someone says that your brilliant life plan isn't going to work, and you need to retool it. Plus, the new tasks we were assigning to them included things they had little experience or confidence in.

I want to be precise about *how* merit matters. There's an annoying phrase, "It's not what you know; it's who you know," that I would like to blow up because it's not true. This phrase implies that competence is irrelevant. Competence is very relevant. By and large, people must be qualified for the work they are doing. There may have been a time when semi-incompetent people could attain success because they came from the right family or class. But that time has long passed. We live in a highly efficient economy, filled with global trade, robotics, and KPIs; it's a place where nonperformers get squeezed out. The only example I can think of illustrating people using connections to get jobs without any real assessment of their skills is in a small number of summer internships for college students. If you're a C-suite executive or on the company's board of directors, you might be able to get your dimwitted kid into an unpaid internship where they will learn nothing. But that's the exception that proves the rule. Relationship building is not in lieu of competence—it has to happen in addition to it.

It's a bummer to be told that no matter how intelligent you are, how hard you work, or how well you've prepared yourself, that you need to connect to people to get to your goal. If you choose not to connect with other people, you will pay a price.

## Truth #2: The Business World Is More Democratic Than You Think

Building professional relationships can seem intimidating, and it's not always easy. It's often not obvious how to do this effectively, especially when you are young, or if you are the first from your family or community to be working in a particular profession. But it's possible.

The U.S. is a very, very democratic society when it comes to social connection. I'm not talking about electoral mapping or how public policy is set. I mean your ability to go up and talk to someone, or to reach out to someone who is outside your existing set of relationships. If you doubt this, ask just about any person who's immigrated from another country. They can see the openness. This openness allows you to try your hand at advancing your career. And since global business culture has a strong stamp of Americanness on it, the American style of networking and relationship building is spreading.

To see what is unique about American business culture, let's start with language. Many languages have two different ways of saying "you." They have a polite, formal version, and a familiar, informal version. In Spanish it's *usted* and *tú*. In French it's *vous* and *tu*. In Chinese it's *nín* (您) and *nǐ* (你). You dance from one to another according to the national culture and situation. You typically start with the polite form until you have permission to or feel comfortable transitioning to the familiar version.

In the U.S., we have just one word for "you." Everyone, regardless of age, wealth, or status gets the same "you," and they use the same "you" with you.[2] You can show someone the deepest respect, but you aren't going to change your form of address.[3]

No one is going to stop you from networking or tell you that you are weird and tacky for trying to meet people you don't already know. You won't necessarily get what you want, but no one will ask you for a permission slip. Introductions are helpful, but in contrast to places like the United Kingdom

---

2. "You" was originally the formal form in English. "Thee," "thou," and "thine" were the traditional informal pronouns. That's why they show up a lot in Christian prayers—your relationship with God is supposed to be intimate and personal. But language changes and now "you" is universal and informal.

3. In other countries where English is spoken, it's not unknown to refer to higher-status people in the third person, rather than saying "you." ("Would the gentleman like to see some more options?" "Would Bibi like another glass of wine?"). And if *Downtown Abbey* is any guide, it wasn't so long ago that this third-person way of addressing someone was used in the United Kingdom, where status differences were present.

and Italy, you do not need to be introduced. You can write an email to a CEO. If you happen to sit next to a celebrity on a plane, you can speak to him or her. It's their choice whether to engage with you, but you've committed no crime. You haven't even committed a faux pas.

And who knows, they may engage with you, even if you're an ordinary person and they are famous and super powerful. After I scored an invitation to the White House Christmas party, some insiders advised me to request a wheelchair for my eighty-plus-year-old mother. This was helpful in itself—the White House is big!—but the other benefit of being in a wheelchair was that my mom could take her place in a special roped-off section in the presidential receiving line. As the Obamas made their way down the line, I whispered to my mother, "Say 'Feliz Navidad' to Michelle Obama. That will get her attention."

The First Lady came by, and my mother cried out, "Feliz Navidad." Ms. Obama's eyes lit up. "Feliz Navidad!" she said, in an excellent accent, taking both my mother's hands into her own. In most countries, random people would not have the opportunity to shake hands with the First Lady.

Not every day is going to be the White House Christmas party. The freedom to *try to access* someone doesn't mean you will succeed in *having access*. People are busy, they have their interests, and they may wish to hang out with people other than you. But in this country and increasingly in many others that are being influenced by American business culture, no one will stop you from trying.

## Truth #3: How You Say Things Matters

Communication is an art. Some types of greetings, introductions, and requests work far better than others. Most people do not communicate as well as they could, and that includes people who went to Harvard Business School.

Communicating effectively benefits from preparation. Winging it might feel authentic, but it rarely accomplishes what you think. When you are connecting in professional relationships, you are trying to be understood in a certain way. You want people to understand your capabilities and interests, your goals and questions, what you're looking for, and what you can offer. This is particularly true when you don't know people very well or have limited time with them.

There is no single solution that will work everywhere. You need nuance, which comes from optimizing the right balance between different conversational choices:

- Being general and being specific
  - "I'm interested in taking my leadership to the next level."
  - "I want to learn negotiation models."
- Asking directly versus expressing needs
  - "Would you be able to introduce me to Channing Dungan?"
  - "I'm working on making connections with senior leaders in television."
- Conveying deference and conveying self-possession
  - "I've followed your career for many years and am aware of your contributions to the field."
  - "I'm extremely organized and reliable, and I know I can add value to this project."
- Sticking to an agenda versus relaxing into a conversation
  - "I'd like to circle back to our second objective. We haven't yet come to a decision on next steps."
  - "What?! You went to Tulum last week? What was your favorite part?"
- Being curious about others and making disclosures about yourself
  - "What didn't you like about public accounting?"
  - "I saw how much my mentor teacher loved her job and realized I shared none of that passion."
- Answering questions directly versus message delivery (this occurs in interviews)
  - "My interest in software design? Since childhood I've been a hacker, always trying to figure out how things fit together . . ."

- — "The drop in our stock price? Brett, I'm going to share with your
    viewers why I believe in this company so much."
- Expressing yourself versus being aware of what the audience is
  experiencing
    - — "Then I got COVID again, and I was more annoyed than any-
      thing else because the custody hearing was coming up . . ."
    - — "I want to pause and ask what you're thinking or feeling right
      now."

Almost everyone can do better, and when you communicate better,
you'll get better results. The sample scripts and exercises in the following
chapters will teach you how to hit the right balance.

## Truth #4: Networks Become More Valuable Over Time

Networks grow and become more valuable over time. The more you invest
now, the greater the benefit will be when you're older.

First, your network will grow since you will continue to meet new people
as you age. People are clustered around institutions and situations: work,
school, neighborhoods, and so on. Each time you enter a new one, you'll
have access to more people with whom you have something specific in common. Social media has made it easier to keep in contact than before. Once
you make a connection on LinkedIn, assuming they stay actively employed,
you'll be able to see what they are up to, no matter how many jobs changes
they make, and vice versa.

Second, your network will have more to offer you as you get older. People tend to become more successful, more influential, and wealthier as they
grow older—not all people, but a lot of them. Their own networks age and
deepen. One of the most powerful groups I've met are women in their fifties
and sixties in New York. They are experienced, know everyone, have strong
social skills, and don't hesitate to connect. (Pro tip: if a professional woman
in this cohort ever offers to take you under her wing, take her up on it!)

Third, as Hollywood television writer Elizabeth Craft says, "People become successful in groups." This just sort of . . . happens. The more present and consistent you are in your invisible network, the more likely success will rub off on you and carry you along.

## Truth #5: Harness the Strength of Weak Ties

"The strength of weak ties" was coined by Mark Granovetter in 1973.[4] Granovetter examined people's personal ties and defined them as "strong" or "weak." He then examined how these worked in job searches.

A weak tie is someone you don't know very well at all or who you once knew but with whom you have fallen out of touch. They don't show up much in your day-to-day life or are somewhat peripheral to your main activities. In contrast, strong ties are people with whom you have ongoing exchanges. You run into them a lot, or it's natural to send them a message, make a call, or stop by their home or office.

You can plot all your contacts as dots in a series of concentric circles—imagine a radar screen or bull's-eye target. Put yourself in the middle, and then arrange people according to how distant they are from you. The further away from you they are, the weaker the tie is. Weak doesn't mean insignificant, unfriendly, or hard to contact. It just means they are less a part of your daily life than strong ties.

Granovetter discovered that people who relied on their weak ties were more successful than people who relied on their strong ties. They got more job offers, with better salaries, and they had greater job satisfaction.

I have seen the power of weak ties play out many times with clients and in my own life, not simply in terms of job search, but also in terms of other goals like business development, fundraising, and even making new friends.

---

4. Mark S. Granovetter, "The Strength of Weak Ties," *American Journal of Sociology* 78, no. 6 (May 1973): 1360–1380, https://www.jstor.org/stable/2776392.

- You work as an engineer, and your family finds your idea of writing a screenplay to be fanciful. Then you take a screenwriting workshop, and classmates find your writing deft and interesting.
- You tell your office tenant that your daughter is applying to prestigious master's programs in cybersecurity. Your tenant points out that if your daughter applies directly to a PhD program, she can probably get full funding, something you had never heard before.
- You mention to a Taiwan-born teacher at your school that your son wants to visit Taiwan for the summer but doesn't have any connections. She writes her brother-in-law, who is a resident at a hospital in Taipei, and your son is offered room and board in exchange for teaching English to the staff.
- You are an endodontist, conducting a root canal on a new patient, and mention that your son and daughter-in-law are anxious about finding a preschool program in New York. Your patient names a Catholic school in their neighborhood that has a great program and costs a small fraction of non-parochial private programs.
- You have been thinking of going to a conference on surrogacy for gay men as a way of taking a step forward in your parenting journey. A new business contact mentions he is going to the same conference, and you decide to attend together.

There are specific reasons why weak ties can be so powerful.

First, it's a numbers game. You might know a fair number of people. But you "kind of know" a lot more. This ratio gets more lopsided as you get older. It also increases as you change environments and develop new interests. The larger size of the weak tie network can lead to more information and more opportunities.

A second reason is that your weak ties have different information than you. People in your immediate circles—in your job, school, and community—often have the same type of information as you do.

For instance, if you are a recent grad and hanging out with other recent grads, you're only getting a small subset of possibly useful information. You're also investing a lot time with other people who are in some sense competing with you. If you branch out to a wider network, you're more likely to come in contact with people who are in different situations from you. They can be helpful without the element of competition. I'd extend this to say that whatever your age, you need to know people from multiple generations. Otherwise, you're stuck in a limited-information band.

Third, weak ties can be supportive of the ways you want to grow and change. They are not attached to a preconceived notion of you. Your strong ties may believe in your strengths, but they also know your weaknesses, or think they do. They can love you, but they can also pigeonhole you. They can have "loving doubts."

Your strong ties may also be threatened if you want to make a change. They may be invested in a particular idea of who you are and what you're supposed to do, including what you're supposed to do for them. Clichés are often borne from truth. The son's desire to go to drama camp conflicts with his jock dad's vision of him playing football. The daughter's desire to go to medical school on the East Coast conflicts with her mom's desire to keep her close to the family in Phoenix. As you progress in your career, your strong ties may want you to stay the way you are right now.

Fourth, weak ties can be safer. If I sit next to a stranger on a plane and mess up when talking about my book idea, who cares? After we change planes, we'll never see each other again. There's less performance anxiety. Toastmasters International operates on this premise. You improve your public speaking skills by practicing with a group of strangers who have nothing to do with your job. You can stammer, stumble, and make a mess of things in a safe environment as you gradually improve your capabilities and confidence.

In most cases, it's easier to refer a weak tie than a strong tie for a job. "Check out the résumé of this cool person I met at the conference" is less weighty than "Check out my brother-in-law's résumé." When you introduce a weak tie, you are offering rather than selling.

We naturally invest a lot of time and care in our strong ties. But when it comes to learning, experimentation, and growth, you need to put energy into your weak ties.

## Truth #6: Make Social Contagion Work for You

When my sons turned two, I took them to the pediatrician for their regular appointment. I knew that she would check their language development, so I counted up the words they knew. I was attempting to raise them bilingually, and they knew a grand total of twenty-eight words between English and Spanish. Woo-hoo!

Their verbal dexterity did not wow the pediatrician, however. Twenty-eight words was *low*. "We're going to keep watching that," she said, a phrase she would repeat in the coming years for a range of developmental targets, each repetition causing me to freak out, at least temporarily.

After the appointment, I started doing the panicked online research one does. Nothing made me feel better. Then one day my friend Gretchen said, "Send them to preschool. Kids learn from other kids."

Up to this point, they'd had home caregivers rather than school, since with twins the costs add up differently. I put my sons in a Montessori preschool, and within a matter of months I could not get them to shut up.

*Social contagion*, a term pioneered by Yale researcher Nicholas Christakis, specifically refers to the ways that social networks transmit perceptions and behaviors, and my kids' experience in Montessori preschool was a prime example of it. Your decisions and actions are not simply things you think up on your own. What you do is affected by what people around you are doing—not just your friends, but also by your friends' friends' friends.

Social contagion theory holds that phenomena that seem very much matters of personal volition, such as losing weight, smoking, getting vaccinated, voting, charitable giving, and speed of walking, are all likely affected by what people in your network are doing. It's osmotic learning. What the people around you are doing, you're probably going to end up doing as well.

When you think about changing your life, the natural thing to do is to name your goal and write action steps. A different way of thinking is to focus on changing your network and let the rest just happen. This is what every concerned parent knows when they want their teenager to hang out with a different crowd. Peer groups define what is normal and what is possible.

You can harness the power of social contagion. Whatever your goal, find a network of people who have a similar goal, and then *start spending more time with them.* You could hang out with knitters, ice fishing fans, or tiny-house owners. Whatever suits your fancy. You can start by doing it in person or virtually.

These are the six truths of how we can interact with weak ties and total strangers in ultimately positive ways. In the next chapter, we'll examine how you create a system for engaging with this world of possibility.

## TWENTY-MINUTES-A-DAY EXERCISES

- **Exercise 1: Weak tie listing.** Take a blank piece of paper and draw a large circle. Draw two concentric circles inside it. This is your network map. You are at the center. (You can download a version of this at michaelmelcher.com and click the "Resources" tab.) Set a timer and spend fifteen minutes writing down the names of your contacts, using their placement to indicate how strong or weak they are.
- **Exercise 2: Assessing weak ties.** Looking at the drawing you made in Exercise 1 and write answers to the following questions: (1) What are the strengths of my network? (2) What are the weaknesses? (3) With

whom do I want to invest more time? (4) Do these people represent any specific category for me?

- **Exercise 3: Applying social contagion.** (1) Ask yourself, "What are the categories of people I *would like to* hang out with more?" Consider personalities, professions, and identities. (2) Do a second version of the radar screen with only names in these categories. (3) Brainstorm how you can invite yourself more into that world—consider people, events, books, podcasts, and so on.

# CHAPTER 4
# Planning Your Relationship Portfolio

E ven in high school, TaTy'Terria Gary was well known in her home city of Topeka, Kansas. She was ambitious, friendly, and took advantage of every opportunity. She seemed to be in every school club and was president of many of them. She attended enrichment programs on the side and was active in her church. And all this as an introvert.

A higher-education reporter for the *New York Times*, Anemona Harto-collis, had also attended Topeka High School a couple of decades before. She returned in 2016 to write on the subject of "Why college?"[1] Topeka, a small city in the middle of the country, seemed representative of much of America. TaTy was chosen to be part of the profile, and her photo ended up on the cover of the *Times*. The story described her accomplishments and drive, and also the challenges she faced. TaTy was from a low-income family where no one had gone to college. She had excellent grades, but her standardized test

---

1. Anemona Hartocollis, "College Is the Goal. Will These Three Teenagers Get There?," *New York Times*, October 25, 2016, https://www.nytimes.com/interactive /projects/cp/national/college-applications.

scores were not high enough to qualify for admission to some of the large schools she was interested in. Before going to college, she had never owned a laptop—she wrote all her high school papers on her phone. The story was inspiring and heartrending. I read it on the edge of my seat.

Many other *Times* readers had reactions similar to mine, because a number of them reached out to Hartocollis, as well as to Helen Crow, a real estate agent in Topeka named in the article who had taken on the role of mentor and small-scale philanthropist for various causes in the city. Thirty-eight individuals from around the country made contributions, and around twenty-five people became part of an online support group for TaTy. It's a group that has persisted for more than five years, as TaTy has gone through college at Newman University in Wichita and into a master's program in genetic counseling at Bay Path University in Longmeadow, Massachusetts. One result of this support is that TaTy finished her undergraduate education debt free. But more than anything, the group has been an ardent cheerleading squad for TaTy, thrilling in her accomplishments and marveling in her growth. Around once a month, TaTy sends an update to Helen Crow, who forwards it to the group.

You can imagine that keeping in touch with this group of *New York Times*–reading fans could be a good thing for TaTy as she moves forward in life. But these aren't the only relationships TaTy has. She has professors and mentors from college. She has supervisors from clinical rotations in grad school. She met people when she took on various leadership roles. She is still in contact with her first mentors from the enrichment program she did in high school. She shares a strong Christian faith with many others. She has worked a dozen jobs. She has classmates, friends, and family. And she's still in her early twenties.

How should she manage all these relationships going forward—and figure out which new ones to build? And how should she do this in her spare time? She is a busy person.

Everyone faces a version of TaTy's challenge. There are *a lot* of people you can potentially connect and reconnect with. How do you decide with whom, and when? If you have fifteen or twenty free minutes, do you know how you will spend that time?

At root, there are two things you need to figure out:

1. Who do you need to connect with?
2. Who do you need to connect with right now?

Once you've thought this through ahead of time, you can be more effective and have less anxiety.

## The Relationship Portfolio

Let's start with a finance analogy. Good investment managers don't advise you to buy a particular stock. They advise you to assemble a portfolio that represents your financial needs based on your stage of life and appetite for risk. A financial portfolio includes countercyclical elements. Focusing on the performance of a portfolio is different from focusing on a single stock.

You need a relationship portfolio—not just one type of relationship. You will build this portfolio, monitor it, maintain it, and leverage it. It will take some time to get going, but ultimately it will be a major part of your life.

The core categories of your relationship portfolio are:

- Weak ties
- Sponsors and mentors
- Colleagues at work
- Bosses and senior stakeholders
- Clients and customers
- Friends
- Beneficiaries

I'll explain what each of these is.

**Weak ties.** This is the biggest category in your invisible network. These are people you don't know well, or at all, or who you once knew but have fallen out of touch with. Weak ties surface opportunities, give you new information, and support change. But there's almost always discomfort in reaching out to weak ties since, by definition, you don't have an ongoing exchange with them.

Also, because there are a lot of them, you will never be able to connect with all of them in one fell swoop. But we can create a method where you will steadily connect with a great number of them over time.

**Sponsors and mentors.** These are people who take a keen interest in your career and want you to succeed. They connect you with people, make introductions, and sometimes intervene in decisions. Mentors share their own experiences and wisdom and answer your questions. They provide important technical knowledge and give context. You want to focus on finding mentors and building those relationships, and then over time turning some of these mentors into sponsors.

**Colleagues at work.** Your work colleagues might be in your department, down the hall, or across the globe. Their function might be completely different from yours. Because most people don't choose their workplace colleagues, they often assume that these relationships don't count. They do! Your ability to succeed in your job depends a lot on how healthy your workplace relationships are.

Too many workplace relationships are transactional: you call the person when you need the thing, and vice versa. What you need are healthy, mutually beneficial relationships that exist beyond specific asks or required interactions. You want a reservoir of mutual understanding and respect.

**Bosses and senior stakeholders.** Your boss is a person with interests and needs. They exist on various ranges: from inspiring to ho-hum, from involved to absent, from kind to irascible. You might have multiple bosses. Whatever their characteristics, they are important to your career. They delegate to you, teach you, and evaluate you. Bosses are also likely to be a source of mentorship and sponsorship. You can learn more from a great boss than from nearly anyone else.

Your work is to build relationships with bosses and senior stakeholders so that your interaction is more than you just reporting results to them or receiving evaluations from them. There is an element of hierarchy in these relationships, but they are still reciprocal and follow the rules of other relationships.

**Clients.** In many professions, clients determine whether you live or die as an enterprise. Sometimes your clients are called something different, but for our purposes, the client is the person who relies on your work. Clients can have a lot of power, but they are human beings who have human needs.

Your client relationships cannot be an afterthought. Your success depends on building positive relationships with them. This means not just providing results but also understanding them.

**Friends.** Your friends can be people you enjoy hanging out with. They can be cheerleaders. They can be givers of tough love. They can be people who get where you are coming from—no explanation or translation necessary. Maybe you have the same lived experiences, or maybe you are quite different but click well.

According to Gallup, Inc., creators of the popular CliftonStrengths (formerly StrengthsFinder) tool, one of the most important measurements of workplace satisfaction is whether you have a best friend at work.[2] More broadly, your positive relationships with people who understand you and whom you personally care about make a big difference in happiness.

We naturally gravitate toward friends, yet we rarely place them front and center as part of our career strategy. These types of people *want* us to connect with them and use their energies, but we often don't.

---

2. Alok Patel and Stephanie Plowman, "The Increasing Importance of a Best Friend at Work," Gallup, August 17, 2022, https://www.gallup.com/workplace/397058 /increasing-importance-best-friend-work.aspx.

**Beneficiaries.** From the beginning of your career, you have the power to make a positive difference in the careers and lives of others. You already know useful things and have useful connections. You don't have to wait to be a benefactor; you can do it right now.

Being a benefactor changes the way you view yourself and strengthens your sense of personal power. It makes your invisible network a place where there is a balance between giving and receiving. It ends up making it easier for you to ask for what might help you.

These are the main categories. You need to invest in all of them. You don't have to do it all at once, but over time you want to do your best for each category. Together, they will fill out your invisible network.

## Using the Relationship Portfolio Bingo Card

We can visually represent your relationship portfolio in a dynamic way with an interactive bingo card that lists all the core categories while letting you set goals each month for how you want to interact with people.

Below is a description of how the bingo card works. To download or print out the actual interactive spreadsheet, go to my website, michaelmelcher .com, and click on the "Resources" tab. And if you prefer to use pen and paper, you can jot down the categories and identify who will be in each.

There are sixteen squares on the bingo card. These are for the relationships you want to be *intentional* about this month. Sixteen is intended to stretch you without being overwhelming. You will likely interact with more people than sixteen in any given month, but again, these are the ones you are trying to be intentional about.

For convenience, I've chosen a monthly cadence. You could do shorter or longer timespans (for example, each week or every two months), but months work pretty naturally in our calendar. There are times you might want to increase your activity level: for example, if you are aggressively looking for a new job, if you are trying to raise funds for a new business, or if you are in a new sales or business development role.

Here is what the basic bingo card looks like.

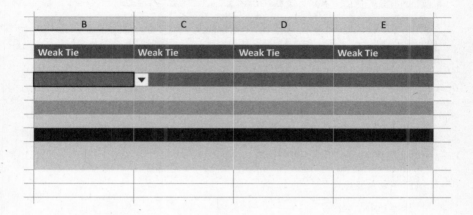

The first four rows are defined as weak ties, because you need at least four of these per month or cycle.

Each of the other cells has a drop-down menu that allows you to label each cell in the desired category:

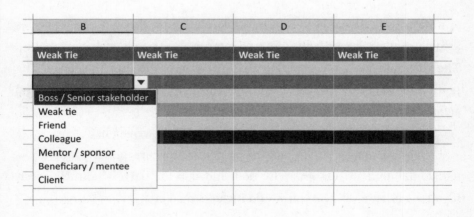

Label each cell and then fill in the cell under each label with names of people you are going to focus on. Here's my example for this month:

| B | C | D | E |
|---|---|---|---|
| Weak Tie | Weak Tie | Weak Tie | Weak Tie |
| Robert O. | S. Smith | Brian S. | C. Munoz |
| Weak Tie | ▼ lleague | Colleague | Beneficiary / mentee |
| N. Feldman | Kimberly | Peter | Marisabel |
| Client | Client | Client | Client |
| Dan S. | Stacy | Steve | Jennifer J. |
| Friend | Friend | Friend | Mentor / sponsor |
| Joy L. | Stacey Schwartz | Kurt Fulepp | P. McLean |

You can see that I've identified:

- Five weak ties
- Two colleagues
- One beneficiary
- Four clients
- Three friends
- One mentor/sponsor
- Zero bosses/senior stakeholders

Many of these could fit into multiple categories. Some of my weak ties are friends I rarely see. Some of my clients are also friends. It doesn't matter. The basic purpose is to generate a range of names to give you focus. The point isn't to get the perfect plan, just *a* plan to channel your energy and actions this month.

Again, if you prefer pen and paper, you can just write a list.

I'm going to have you fill out the bingo card for this month. If you know who to put on it already, great. Go do it and skip the next section. However, if you're not sure yet who you would include, read on.

## Identify the (Potential) People in Your Portfolio

We'll generate names through a few different exercises.

## Exercise 1: Work Stakeholder Mapping

Answer the following questions to map and identify your key work stakeholders.

### Bosses and Stakeholders

1. Who is your boss (or your bosses)?
2. Who else is involved in evaluating your work or weighing in on your promotion and compensation?

### Clients, Customers, and External Stakeholders

3. Who are some of your important clients or customers?
4. Who are some other external stakeholders?

### Direct Reports and Support People

5. Who are your direct reports?
6. For whom else do you play a role in providing opportunities or evaluating work?
7. Who inside your company or organization helps you get your job done?
8. What outside vendors or consultants contribute to you getting your work done?

### Lateral Relationships

9. Who works with you in a lateral capacity (neither of you manages the other)?
10. What other departments or offices do you connect with from time to time?

### Workplace Friends and Supporters

11. Who are your work buddies or friends?
12. Who has the ability to be a trusted advisor—whether or not they are a friend?

**Special Cases**

13. Who at work would you like to know better, if you could figure out a way to do so?

14. With whom at work do you have negative energy? (This is not about assigning blame—think about which relationships occupy some negative space in your head.)

15. Who are your mentors or sponsors in the workplace?

16. Who is someone at work you are helping out?

## Exercise 2: Outside of the Workplace

Answer the following questions to come up with additional people you know.

**Friends**

1. Who are some key friends you see regularly?

2. Who are five friends you like but haven't spoken to for a while?

3. Who is someone who can give you tough love (and whose tough love you will accept)?

**Mentors and Sponsors**

4. Who are mentors or sponsors you have outside of your workplace?

5. Who is someone intriguing (and not currently a mentor or sponsor) who you feel you could learn from?

**Former Colleagues, Bosses, or Clients**

6. Who is a former boss you are on good terms with?

7. Who are some former clients you have positive regard for?

8. Who are some former colleagues worth knowing?

**Professional Connections**

9. Who are some people in your field you respect?

10. Who is someone far older or more experienced with whom you are connected?

11. Who is someone in your field at a similar level who is probably dealing with similar issues as you?

12. Who is someone in your field with whom you feel a strong identity match?

13. Who is someone quite different from you with whom you nonetheless have positive energy?

14. Who is someone well networked in professional organizations?

### Beneficiaries

15. Who is someone you have mentored or could mentor?

16. What's an organization you have supported financially or in some other way?

17. Who is someone you've met through volunteering, civic work, or board service?

## Exercise 3: "Someone Who" Exercise

Here is a different set of prompts to stimulate your memory. This is the most popular exercise from my previous book, *The Creative Lawyer*, with some minor modifications.

Write the name of someone you know who:

1. Knows how to have fun _____

2. Knows everyone _____

3. Can give you encouragement in tough times _____

4. Will give you tough talk _____

5. Is consistently logical _____

6. Is deeply empathetic _____

7. Is spiritually advanced _____

8. Can handle a crisis _____

9. Has known you since childhood _____

10. Is politically connected _____

11. Is entrepreneurial _____

12. Is good at raising kids _____

13. Is an expert on money _____

14. Is an expert on relationships _____

15. Is an expert on health _____

16. Is an expert at work/life balance _____

17. Is an expert in the type of work you do _____

18. Is an expert in a type of work you are interested in _____

19. Gives good advice about office politics _____

20. Gives good advice about professional development _____

21. Thinks you are basically great _____

22. Thinks you are capable of more _____

## Exercise 4: Relationship Portfolio Bingo Card

Fill out your bingo card. (Remember, you can find an interactive version at michaelmelcher.com and clicking on the "Resources" tab.) You can also fill out the categories below:

| Category | Names | Total |
|---|---|---|
| Weak ties | (minimum of four) | |
| Bosses/senior stakeholders | | |
| Friends | | |
| Colleagues | | |
| Mentors/sponsors | | |
| Beneficiaries | | |
| Clients | | |
| | Total | 16 |

## TWENTY-MINUTES-A-DAY EXERCISES

- **Exercise 1:** Work through Exercises 1 through 3 in this chapter if you haven't done so already. These might take you a couple of Twenty-Minute sessions.
- **Exercise 2:** Fill out your Relationship Portfolio Bingo Card for this month.

# PART 2
# Creating and Maintaining Relationships

# CHAPTER 5

# You Go First: How to Reach Out

M ihai Ionescu grew up in a provincial city in Romania. At the time
of his birth in 1987, his native country was part of the Soviet Bloc.
By the time he entered elementary school, Romania was a different country from the place his parents had been raised. It was no longer a dictatorship and no longer closed off from the West. Romania was an in-between place. While it had changed, growing up there wasn't the same as growing up in Western Europe or North America. Mihai sensed there were opportunities outside Romania, but he wasn't sure exactly what they were or where he could find them.

He knew that education was a key to progress, and he was good academically. He attended a selective school that focused on math and science. When he was in high school, a boy a couple of years older won a full scholarship to an international boarding school. He came back home after his first summer abroad and gave Mihai the lowdown. This was a chain of schools located all around the world. Students would go there for twelfth and thirteenth grade as an international living experience—each school had students representing around sixty countries. Everyone was on a full scholarship. Soon, Mihai won one of the spots for Romania. A few months later, in the fall of 2004, he flew to the American Southwest.

Mihai continued to excel academically. In science and math, he towered above most of his classmates. He was good at languages as well. He spoke English, Russian, and Romanian, and he picked up Spanish easily.

Culturally, things were more complex.

"When I arrived, I was very Romanian," he recalled. "I was judgmental and probably cynical. I'd never been in a diverse cultural situation." He was, however, very curious, especially about the ways students from different cultures approached life. He dated a Burmese classmate who'd grown up in Singapore and was struck by her "activation energy."

"She would just try things. She'd be curious about something, and she would just go out and try to get it. She'd identify what she wanted and backtrack to figure out how to get it. She was open to changing herself and her life. In contrast, I had some friends from Eastern Europe who just leaned into who they were already. They didn't take risks. I didn't initially have a lot of activation energy, but I gradually developed it."

Activation energy is different from persistence or ongoing effort. It's the energy of initiating things, changing from stationary to moving. Once things get rolling, they often keep rolling.

Mihai went to college in the U.S. and has worked here for the past dozen years. He's currently employed at a large Silicon Valley company in their strategy analytics group. If you didn't know his story, when you consider his career or travels, you might assume he has been all activation energy, all the time, since childhood. But it's really something he developed.

Getting the best from your relationships requires your activation energy. Tapping into your invisible network starts with reaching out. Reaching out is inviting the world to join you. It's rolling up the shutters of your café and putting out an "open" sign. It's going into the elevator with a smile at whoever is there, rather than looking for a safe corner to stare into.

You're going to go first. You're the one who wants to make your career better.

In this chapter, we'll go into how exactly you take the initiative. We will talk about the attitudes that enable you to do this, and then go over what to say to people.

## Getting a Positive-Reinforcement Loop Started

People often feel weird reaching out. So I'm going to tell you something straight-up and early: Your feelings don't matter. Don't be in awe of your feelings. Feel as weird as you want. You are still able to make things happen even while feeling weird.

All kinds of feelings can come up when you start the process of reaching out, from "I don't know what to say," to "I feel embarrassed," to "They'll think I'm weird," to "I wish I were a different kind of person." Whatever you are feeling, it's likely to change once you actually connect with people. Reaching out may seem artificial, but interacting with real people won't.

Some of the people you reach out to will respond. Some of them will agree to speak with you. Some will be excited you reached out. They will recognize your bids and respond to them. You will have real interactions. And some of those conversations will feel good. You will get positive energy back from others. You might start hearing messages that sound like:

- "Sure, we can have a call. I have time tomorrow, if that's not too soon."
- "I'm glad you reconnected. I was just thinking of you a couple of weeks ago."
- "Have you heard of the Op-Ed Project? They have amazing open-enrollment courses."
- "I can totally see you running your own business. You have so many gifts."

- "Hollywood [or finance, or publishing, or sales] is all about rejection. Rejection here isn't even rejection. It's just part of the journey. It's nothing to get bent out of shape about. What you're going through is par for the course."
- "You're asking questions I wish I had asked at your age."
- "I was even older than you when I immigrated to this country. Don't let anyone stop you from going for what you want."

When you actually connect with people, you will initiate a positive-reinforcement loop through which you'll get useful ideas, helpful feedback, new connections, and, ultimately, real opportunities. Other people will contribute to your progress in ways you can't now see. And the way you feel at the beginning will not be how you will feel later on.

## Attitudes That Work

Psychological research has documented that feelings follow thoughts, not the other way around. If you think something will suck, then you will feel it sucking. If you think you will enjoy something, you will feel enjoyment. If you say, "I can handle this," you are more likely to feel yourself handling it. This goes against the grain of modern life, where we spend a lot of time analyzing our feelings as a source of wisdom. I have as many of the feels as anyone, and I am comfortable asserting that sometimes feelings are stupid. If you change your thoughts, you change your feelings, and then you change your actions.

This is where affirmative beliefs, mindsets, core principles, and even mantras come in. Taking on any challenge is easier when you set forth some core principles that you believe in, or try to believe in, as guideposts on a path toward positive action. Every successful self-help program in the world has these. Alcoholics Anonymous has its twelve steps, and Weight Watchers has its principles of change.

When it comes to activating your invisible network, there are three core attitudes that will make reaching out easier for you.

The first is a **spirit of generosity**. This means *your* generosity. You assume that speaking to people is worth your time. You are willing to spend time and energy doing this that you would otherwise use for different things. You're ready to go for it, generally, and you don't spend a lot of time parsing things on a case-by-case basis, assessing whether this or that person really merits a reach-out. You're willing to be a bit promiscuous.

I can easily spot when clients lack this spirit of generosity. They ask a lot of questions about how long things will take and whether this will really work. They want a guarantee that things are worth it before they make the effort.

The second is a **spirit of curiosity**. You adopt a beginner's mind, which means "I know very little" rather than "I know most things." When you contemplate reaching out, you make a practice of *wondering*: I wonder what I'll learn from this person. I wonder what this conversation will be like. You walk in as a learner, not as an expert.

The third is a **spirit of prosperity**. The professional world isn't *The Hunger Games*. There's no scarcity of worthwhile people. There are billions of people out there, and you only need to meet a tiny fraction of them. There's a lot of success possible, and you only need to have your bit. If other people win, you can win as well, and vice versa. It's not a zero-sum game.

## Reaching Out for a Specific Need Versus Reaching Out as an Ongoing Practice

Reaching out can be sorted into two broad categories. The first is for a specific need. The second is as an ongoing practice.

When you have a need, you are seeking a solution of some kind. You could be seeking help, advice, feedback, agreement to do something, a referral or connection, a donation, or almost anything else. You can seek this solution in a relationship-building and relationship-respecting way, but you do want something, and probably now.

When you are reaching out as an ongoing practice, you are focusing on developing the relationship itself. You don't have a specific need, or it's a longer-term thing, or the "need" is a device you use to build the connection. For instance, a mom in the neighborhood stopped by my apartment to drop off two uninflated soccer balls from a big consignment she'd received for a program her kids were in. I didn't need soccer balls, and I don't think she perceived that I really needed them, but it was a nice thing to do, and it took our relationship a small step farther.

The more you make your reaching out a practice rather than something in response to specific needs, the stronger your invisible network will be in the long run. But don't get too bent out of shape if you mainly connect with people when you have specific needs.

| **Reaching Out for a Specific Need**<br>(You have a problem to solve or are looking for a specific outcome from a specific interaction.) | **Reaching Out as an Ongoing Practice**<br>(You are building or maintaining your relationship.) |
| --- | --- |
| • Looking for advice or a recommendation<br>• Getting feedback<br>• Learning something specific<br>• Trying to make other connections<br>• Introducing a client to a service<br>• Making a sale<br>• Seeking a donation<br>• Educating a business prospect about what you do<br>• Checking up on a prospect | • Building a new relationship<br>• Reconnecting with a past relationship<br>• Updating contact info<br>• Sharing what your job is now<br>• Learning more about the other person<br>• Sharing more about yourself<br>• Finding people or interests in common<br>• Reminding people you exist<br>• Sharing information they might find useful<br>• "Pinging" |

## Scripts for Reaching Out

### Brand-New Connection

You've met someone. Now you want to keep it moving along.

**LinkedIn Connection Request**
- "Hey Joy—it was nice to see you on the Zoom call yesterday. Would love to stay in touch."

**Email or Text**
- "Hey Joy—it was great meeting you at Sasha's event. I'd love to stay connected. Texting so you have my number! —Jerome"
- "Hey Joy—it was great meeting you at Sasha's event. Here is the article I mentioned about work/life balance—it talks about energy management, and I found it really helpful. Let's stay in touch. —Jerome"

**Voicemail or Voice Memo**
- "Hey Joy—just wanted to follow up to say it was great to meet you. We may see each other at Sasha's next event, but in the meantime, you can reach me at this number."

### Brand-New Not-Quite-Connection

Sometimes you'll be at the same event as someone but not get the chance to speak with them. You can still use the event as a reason to connect.

**Email or LinkedIn Message**
- "Hello, Michael! I really enjoyed your presentation at Jennie Nash's book coaching event. I didn't ask any questions, but I was riveted. Would love to connect with you/keep in touch. —Jennifer"

## Following Up on a Referral

People may suggest you meet someone. It's nice when they formally introduce you, but you can follow up on your own. You want to name the connection, explain briefly who you are, and explain why you'd like to speak with them.

**Email: Informational Interview**
Subject line: Referral from Josh Maitra

Dear Priya,

I was given your name by Josh Maitra. I have known Josh for a few years, and he has been a great resource on career tips as well as being a good friend.

I'm exploring entry-level positions in television production, including production assistant jobs. I've found it very helpful to speak to people who have gotten their start in television in these positions. I'm learning more about what's expected and what to do (and not do) in the first months on the job. Would you have fifteen minutes to chat? I know you are super busy and most likely get requests like this all the time, but your time would be much appreciated.

Best Regards,
Michael Melcher

**Email: Advice About Wedding Planning**
Subject line: Referral from Trish Przska (re: wedding planning)

Dear Jackie,

We are both friends of Trish. We used to be on the same swim team as kids back in Atlanta.

I have a wedding coming up in a year and was venting to Trish about how I don't even know where to start. She said that you are the most organized person she knows and handled your own wedding with aplomb, and suggested I reach out. Would you have fifteen minutes to talk to a newbie? I would love your take on what is necessary and what is not.

Best Regards,
Clark

**Email: Early Exploration of Business Opportunities**
Subject: Learning more about L&D at Grayson (Mike Suh referral)

Dear Janice,

Mike Suh suggested I reach out to you. I was speaking to him about doing coaching for managing partners at Grayson and other firms, and he said you are the right person to contact, given that you now run all of L&D at the firm.

I have actually been following your career from a distance for some time now—we have a few friends in common, including Hanna Halspie and Leslie Darcy.

Would you have time for an introductory call in the next few weeks? I'd love to learn more about what your plans are for coaching and leadership development at the firm, and I could share a bit about myself. I'd love to have an initial conversation with you.

Best Regards,
Michael Melcher

## Reconnecting with Someone You've Been Out of Touch With

Of all the Twenty-Minutes-a-Day activities you will do over the years, one of the biggest categories will be reconnecting with people you've been out of touch with. Some of these will be beloved old friends, and others will be people you didn't know all that well to begin with. No matter. You can reach out to everyone just the same.

## Old Friend or Acquaintance, No Specific Ask

### Call or Voicemail

- "Hey Ed. How have you been? I just drove past our old office building and thought of you. I think you might know that I have kids now—twin sons who are in second grade. Anyway, give me a call sometime. I'd love to catch up."

### Email, Text, or Social Media Message

- "Hellooooooooo Courtney. It's Michael. I walked past the café on Columbus where we used to get coffee (back when it cost less than two bucks). Just want to say hi, and I hope things are going great with you. —Michael"

## Old Friend or Acquaintance, With Focus

### Email

Subject line: How many years has it been? / Hello and a question

Hey Louise—I hope you're well. It's been a long time!

I would love to catch up but, in the meantime, have a quick question for you: Who was that career coach you worked with? My husband has been in a funk about his job (which I agree he should leave) but isn't doing much about it. I can't tell him anything but thought another party might have influence. Or maybe the person you worked with knows people.

Your pal,
Shirley


Subject line: It's been a while / Hello and a request

Hey Dorotea—I hope you're well. I can't believe we haven't spoken for five years, but I've been watching your impressive climb from a distance. I was watching *Succession* the other day and thinking, "Dorotea could explain all these mysterious financial transactions to me."

Okay, here's a request. My son is a junior at the University of Richmond. He is interested in getting an analyst job on Wall Street. He knows that many New York firms don't recruit at his school and, to his credit, is trying to network. I was wondering . . . would you be able to speak with him for fifteen to twenty minutes? This is not a job request (and he knows that)—more like getting the lay of the land.

Feel free to say no—no obligation, but I just wanted to put it out there.

—Drew

## Weak Tie from the Past (Someone You Never Knew Well)

Subject line: Greetings from your law school classmate; upcoming meeting

Dear Sri,

Hello! It's your law school classmate Michael Melcher. It's been around twenty years since we both sat listening to Prof. Schon's stories.

I've followed your progress from afar and was excited when I heard you were named managing partner. I've been working as an executive coach for the past couple of decades. By coincidence, we are currently pitching a big leadership program for your firm, and I believe we're going to see each other at an upcoming meeting. It will be great to reconnect.

—Michael

Subject line: Greetings from your law school classmate; question about healthcare sector

Dear Edna,

Greetings. I'm not sure if you remember me, but we were in the same small section at Emory. (I was one of the people who sat in the back and never spoke so as not to attract the attention of professors. But I was good listener!)

I've spent fifteen years since graduation in a variety of legal positions (large firms and in-house) and have found a lot of fulfilment in the health-care sector. I'm currently exploring my next steps and am looking at several major hospitals in the Atlanta metro area. Would you have fifteen minutes to chat in the next weeks? Given your own experience at Piedmont, I think I would learn a lot.

–George

## Cold Calls and Emails

A cold call or email is an attempted connection with someone you've never met. This might be someone at a similar level or someone prominent. You will not hit 100 percent in these messages, but you will not hit 0 percent either. The best practices are:

1. Be respectful and slightly deferential, while describing the interest you share;
2. Have a specific request that is easy for them to understand—keep things brief; and
3. Make it easy to say both yes and no. You want to make it easy for them to comply with your request, but you don't want them to feel awkward if they choose not to.

Part of being respectful is showing that you know something about their accomplishments, even if you've never met. Show you've done your homework without being a stalker. Some useful phrases are:

- I've followed your work since . . .
- I learned about you in . . .
- What speaks to me most is . . .
- We have a mutual interest in . . .

**Email: Request of Famous Author**
Subject line: Big fan says hello; be on my podcast?

Dear Meghan Daum,[1]

I read your hilarious novel, *The Quality of Life Report*, when it came out nearly twenty years ago. I then moved on to all your other books. My favorite is your most recent, *The Problem with Everything*.

I'm also a fan of your podcast, *The Unspeakable*. I have a podcast of my own called *Career Stewardship with Michael Melcher*, which shares ideas and models from my experience in executive coaching. Periodically I host episodes where I do actual coaching. I recently listened to your episode on making your transition into podcasting and was wondering: Would you like to be my guest? I would love to do a live coaching session regarding some of your business goals. I think you would find it useful, and it would be fun. What do you think?

–Michael Melcher

**Email: Reaching Out to Respected Leader**
Subject line: An honor to learn about you; potential conversation?

Dear Ms. Torres,

I'm currently a junior at Texas A&M, majoring in political science. I'm also co-chair of Raza, the Mexican-American/Chicano students association.

I recently did a project on prominent Latina leaders, which is how I learned about you and your work for our community and in the White House. I

---

1. This example is modeled after an email I sent to her. I didn't say "Dear Meghan" because it felt overfamiliar—I really do look up to her and I was making a request—and I didn't say "Dear Ms. Daum" because that felt too formal and, based on her writing, didn't match my perception of her style.

immediately FaceTimed my mom y abuelita and told them all about you and showed them your picture.

I know you are very busy and you probably get requests like this all the time, but I'm wondering I could have a twenty-minute conversation with you at your convenience. I would love to get your advice on the best ways to get involved in serving the Latino/a/x community through politics.

Thank you again for all you have done for our community.

Un abrazo,
Alma Benavides

**Email: Request of Prominent Researcher**
Subject line: Admiration for your work; Reaching out from S.B.C. Bank

Dear Prof. Ely,

My name is Antonio Chang, and I'm part of my firm's committee on Diversity, Equity, Inclusion, and Belonging. My regular job is in commercial credit.

We recently used your video talk with Ellen Bailey, "Getting Serious About Diversity," to stimulate a broader discussion with our directors about creating a culture that allows everyone to thrive. It was a really great conversation!

First, thank you for that video and for all your work.

Second, our firm is very global, and I am wondering if you can recommend any Harvard case studies about dealing with international diversity in the workplace.

Third, can you tell us what your speaking fees are, or who I would contact to get that information? Even though we are a bank, we don't have a large budget, but we would love to find a way for you to speak directly with our leaders, perhaps in a simple Q&A session.

Best Regards,
Antonio Chang

## TWENTY-MINUTES-A-DAY EXERCISES————————

- **Exercise 1:** Using one of the scripts as a guide, reach out to a weak tie.
- **Exercise 2:** Using another of the scripts as a guide, reach out to a weak tie.
- **Exercise 3:** Write (and send) an email to a prominent person you admire.

# CHAPTER 6

# Minute 32 and What You Can Expect from a Conversation

Anjali Sinha felt stuck and bored with her career in a big bank. She specialized in change management but was ready for a change herself. She'd been ready for some kind of change for *years*. She needed to figure out either what other job she could do or how she could be more effective and happier in her current job.

She started reaching out to her network, starting with people who seemed easier or lower risk. After a few conversations, she was getting the hang of things, so she began going for more consequential names. One of these was her former boss, Gwen, a woman Anjali admired but whom she had always found intimidating. Anjali hoped that Gwen, as an insider, might have some tips for navigating the system. She rewrote her initial email several times, concerned about getting the right tone. She feared the conversation would be awkward. She did not feel confident. Gwen seemed so different from her. Gwen had it all together.

Gwen agreed to a meeting. From the moment they sat down, the conversation flowed easily. Gwen was surprisingly open. Though Anjali saw

Gwen as a lifer, Gwen actually had strong reservations about the future direction of the firm. She advised Anjali to look for an exit strategy, explaining that the promotion path in their division was congested due to factors that had nothing to do with Anjali. Gwen also shared that she had been on her own quest. She had her own career advisor, had gotten seriously into mind/body health, and wasn't anything like the corporate loyalist that Anjali had assumed she was. She told Anjali that she was asking exactly the right questions at exactly the right time—Anjali was senior enough to have something to offer, yet not so senior that building a career at a new place would be hard. Gwen welcomed her to come back to her for future conversations and references.

Anjali left that meeting pumped up!

Over the next year, she zigzagged toward a new understanding of what might be her next act. She ended up creating a new COO role for herself inside her existing firm and was psyched about the potential. This was a positive result that she never would have imagined when she was getting ready for that first conversation with her former boss.

Anjali's experience happens more frequently than you might think. You can't predict where conversations will go. Some will take off in a marvelous direction, and others will never get off the ground. You cannot avoid this randomness, nor should you try to. Instead, you need to think of it as something for you to manage, where you are intentional yet open to unexpected outcomes. One way you manage it is by staying in the conversations long enough for good things to happen—a point I'll call Minute 32. This chapter is about the unpredictable benefits of conversations and the practices you can follow to maximize the likelihood that they emerge.

## Cocreation Equals Randomness

Actual communication between human beings has a flow that goes beyond logic or plans, even when you have a clear agenda. When we interact, there's the potential that 1 + 1 = 3. Or maybe 7. Or 23.

Human beings are fundamentally creative—and fundamentally co-creative. You say something, and what you say triggers thoughts, feelings, and connections in the other person's brain. They share something back, and that triggers ideas in your own head. And so on.

When you talk to anyone, you aren't just finding things in common. You are also creating something together. You exchange thoughts. You bounce and toss and bat ideas around. You argue and dispute. You say, "Yes, and . . ." You might interrupt and finish each other's sentences. You might reflect on what the other person is saying or get distracted by something you just thought of.

A conversation is never just what is in your own head. Conversations are chemistry in action. The result of two people talking is invisible until it happens. It's not so much waiting to be discovered as it's waiting to be created.

## Reality Check: How Frequently Do Great Conversations Happen?

Your conversations will not be predictable. That doesn't mean they will *all* be amazing. They won't. Let's set expectations.

I recommend you plan for a ratio of 30:50:20. This means that for every ten conversations you have, you can expect that three will be really useful, five will be okay but unexciting, and two may be a waste of time. This applies to job searches, business development, making professional connections, and every other kind of interaction. The size of the buckets may vary a bit, but there will always be the same three buckets.

If you were planning to bat one thousand when you talk to people, this ratio will seem like drag. But it's realistic. There is also freedom in this ratio. It means that if you just do the work, you will end up with results. It's like dating; you are better off having a good dating process than obsessing about how any individual date will work out.

This ratio helps you turn around the meaning of the occasional awkward, dull, or just plain bad conversation. Each time this happens, put a mental notch on your list: you are one step closer to a really great conversation that will get results.

## Minute 32

The real value of a conversation emerges around Minute 32. By that point, you've run through the initial agenda, you've both relaxed into speaking, your synapses have had a chance to warm up and start free-associating, your defenses are down, and one or both of you may have started showing vulnerability.

Minute 32 is a stand-in for the point when unexpected ideas begin flowing. "You know, I just remembered that I know someone . . ." "It just struck me that . . ." "I don't know if this is useful but . . ." You can't precisely foresee what those ideas will be. They might relate to your agenda or to something else. This can happen in any conversation, not just those with new connections.

Assuming we're having a conversation, there are various kinds of things you and I might discover after Minute 32:

- We discover we have something in common: we both lived in Scottsdale, or you have a gay sister, or we both loved *Succession*.
- I provide some useful knowledge or insight: it sounds like they have an inside candidate; that organization just lost a big funding source; it's normal for hiring in nonprofits to take this long.
- I recall contacts that didn't initially come to mind: my roommate from twenty-five years ago; the guy I know who coaches in banking and private equity; the person I met a couple of months ago who works in voter registration.
- You discover that you can help me in unexpected ways: you've been to that resort before; your brother is a neonatologist; you know a much better Mexican restaurant in the same neighborhood.
- You reveal goals that weren't in your initial agenda: you're not sure you really want to become partner; big city life is getting to you; you think you might need to switch your practice area.

- You discover a mutual friend or acquaintance: "You know Phuong from a political campaign? That's so weird. I know Phuong because we went to the same summer enrichment program in junior high."
- You discover information that could benefit someone else you know, or you know a resource that might help me or someone else: "My client's wife is a recruiter for start-ups." "My son went to a great therapist for some sensory issues."
- And so on.

I can't guarantee that Minute 32 is the *exact* moment things will break through. The moment might come after eight minutes or it could come after several hours. Minute 32 is a stand-in for this *stage* of the conversation. It occurs when you don't expect anything to occur. It's the invisible part of the conversation—beyond what you have foreseen.

Beyond chemistry, there are specific reasons why the good parts don't happen right away:

- People warm up at different speeds and in different ways. Some people are ready to hug you the first time you meet, and other people will never hug you.
- People have different ways of hearing, holding, and processing information. Some folks react, process, and move quicky to the next thing, and others let things simmer.
- People rarely have surface access to the full range of information and connections they have. I think I'm pretty sharp, but in some ways my mind is a big, dusty file room. It can take time to find the thing I'm looking for; I might have forgotten I even have it.
- It takes time to build trust, and it also takes time to build *cognition*. I may want to get a real sense of you and process what you are presenting before I reveal what I know.
- If you want advice about a problem, you may be starting with a "presenting issue" rather than the real issue. You're not actually naming

the right issue, even though you think you are. It might take some back-and-forth to land on the right thing.

- People can help in a variety of ways—sometimes quite differently from what you expect. This happens all the time in job searches. You want a lead to a specific company, and instead you get feedback about your résumé. You want to learn about someone's career path, and instead they introduce you to someone else. You want sympathy, and instead they tell you about a conference you've never heard of.

- The conversation isn't over when it's over. Your contacts may speak about you with others later on. What you've talked about will then fuel these later conversations. You won't know the value right away.

I see examples of the surprises of conversations all the time—with my clients and in my own life. In each case, I couldn't predict what was going to happen.

**The Michigan connection.** One of my former clients, Lauren Baer, decided to run for Congress. I was very excited about this and decided to raise money for her, even though I'd never been good at this before. I approached a wealthy man I know who I was pretty sure gave regularly to Democratic causes. I asked him if he would speak with Lauren. He explained he didn't give in primaries but that, with that understanding, he would consider meeting her.

During their meeting, they discovered they were both University of Michigan loyalists. I didn't realize how passionate he was about that school, and I had no idea that Lauren had family connections there since she went to a totally different college and law school and grew up in Florida. He ended up being a big supporter of her race and hosted his own events for her.

**The mom who knows schools.** When my twins were infants, a lot of people came to visit me, including Susan, a former client with teenage children. We caught up as I pushed my double stroller around the playground. I slipped that I had gone to an open house for a private school but wasn't sure if I was open to that expense and general weirdness. "You absolutely cannot send your kids to private school!" she exclaimed. "It's a waste of money and they're terrible. My kids have had great experiences in New York public schools, and there are a lot to choose from." This advice took a huge weight off my chest.

**The Africa adventure.** I met a very unhappy lawyer, Barrett, who wanted to get out of law completely. He didn't know if it was possible. He almost hesitated to share his one true passion, because it seemed so unrealistic: to do something in Africa. In fact, I knew two people who were doing just that: Ali, who used to be a law firm partner, and Katerina, who transitioned from a global nonprofit to venture capital in Africa.

Then, a few weeks later, I remembered another person: Michael, a guy in his twenties with whom I'd had one conversation as a favor to his mother; he had been working in Vietnam and wanted to make a move to Africa. He did end up going to Africa, and by weird coincidence (or maybe no coincidence at all), his new organization, One Acre Fund, was trying to professionalize its management and was looking for a grown-up COO type, which my client, Barrett, then became.

We think of coincidences as things that just happen or that we stumble upon. But you could also argue that coincidences are common interests that exist between two people. For the moment they are invisible, but they are waiting to emerge.

Intention is important, but it is only half the equation. The other half is openness and a willingness to be in the moment.

## How to Engineer a Coincidence: Getting the Conversation Started

There are specific techniques you can use for setting these conversations up to be successful, notwithstanding the goal of being open to the serendipity of Minute 32. I call this conversational leadership.

People are often afraid of being too dominant in conversations, but what they should really fear is being wobbly and incoherent. The openings I dread are the ones that start off, "I'd just really like to talk about your path . . ." Or the ones where we engage in small talk for fifteen minutes without any framing whatsoever. You're allowed to set the tone. Trust me; it's okay. No matter how senior, esteemed, or well-paid your counterpart is, you are doing them a favor if you give some direction for the conversation. Basically, you're telling them how to be successful in the conversation, and everyone wants to feel successful.

Here's how you do this:

1. Explain to the other person why you wanted to speak with them.
2. Provide a simple plan for how the conversation can proceed.
3. Ask them if this is the right agenda or if they'd like a different approach.

Here are some examples in different contexts:

**Job Search**

"The pandemic made me take a hard look at my career priorities. I've spent nearly twenty years in the private sector but now am exploring work in the educational space. I know that you made a major change like this several years ago. I'd love to hear what you learned in that process and what advice you might have for someone trying to follow in your footsteps. Does that sound like a good way to start?"

**Relocation and Social Connection**

"Now that my family is relocating from Chicago to Dallas, I'm looking for ways to make connections and get involved at the civic level—and Marjorie says you know everyone. I'd love to hear your thoughts about ways I might start plugging in. Does that work for you?"

### Business Development

"All the business relationships I've had are things that grew over time. I'd like to consider this an initial, getting to know each other meeting. I'd love to start by learning more about your business and some of your priorities going forward, and I have a few specific questions to follow. Then perhaps I could share more about what my firm does. Does that seem like a good approach for you?"

### Career Advancement

"Even though I've been at the firm for ten years, I think I could be more effective—I'd like to get clearer about how the game is played. When we worked together, you always seemed to know exactly how to deal with things, so I naturally wanted to ask you for advice. My thought today is to share a couple of challenges I'm facing at work and get your input, and then ask more generally about where you see me in the next five to ten years. Or we could go in some other direction. What works best for you?"

### Parenting Advice

"My twins are six, and bedtime every night is a battle. You've been one of my greatest supporters, and you also seem really good at being a parent. I'd love your thoughts about techniques I could try or your guesses about what I'm doing wrong. How does that sound?"

This structure works because you are basically taking over a chore—getting things started. The other person may have forgotten why you are meeting, or have only a vague idea, or even be concerned they are not properly prepared. You're alleviating anxiety in a small but important way. And you are still giving them the choice about how to proceed.

This formula also enforces word economy. It helps ensure that the opening to the conversation is just the opening, not a fifteen-minute download from you.

## During the Conversation

Most people handle conversations well once they are kicked off. It's sort of like my approach to going to the gym. I hem and haw about going, but once I'm in there, I'm fine. Here are some additional tips for bringing out the magic.

**Listen more than you talk.** Don't assume you have to fill silent patches. The other person may just be thinking. If you are extroverted like me, you might have to remind yourself to keep listening. In some conversations, I'll silently chant to myself, "Don't talk, don't talk, don't talk."

**You can bounce around but bring back useful threads.** Natural conversations can move from topic to topic (work; life; the menu; things you're both observing; physical sensations like heat, cold, wind) but track back to things of interest. "So interesting about your kitchen renovations. You know, just to get back to what you were saying about presidential appointments . . ."

**Don't hesitate to mix your personal and work lives.** These are not really separate since we work all the time and live all the time. Some people find it much easier to talk about personal things; others are much more comfortable in work matters. Some are open about both. You just have to experiment. Incidentally, most people do really love talking about their children. Men are rarely asked about this, and rarely ask other men, so if you ask a man about his kids, you are probably giving him the chance to express something he isn't often asked about.

**At some point ask, "What else?"** Ask this when you think you're all done. There will be a pause, but it might open new opportunities.

- What other companies should I be looking at?
- What other tips do you have for dealing with twins?
- Who else should I speak with?
- What else should I be asking you?

Then force yourself to be silent. A good way to do this is to sit on your hands or imagine sitting on your hands.

## Ending the Conversation

**Stay aware of the time.** This is a basic courtesy. Just because the other person seems enchanted by you doesn't mean they aren't busy. "We're almost at thirty minutes, and I want to thank you for taking the time." They might answer, "Oh, no, it's fine." Only continue if they insist or reassure you that it's fine to keep talking.

**Summarize what you got out of the conversation.** You can just mention one or two key things. "You've given me a lot to think about." "I never knew about these three companies; thanks for alerting me to those." It shows you have been listening and it will be interesting for them to hear what you are taking away.

**Clarify any action steps.** This reminds them of any commitments and reinforces any offers of help. "I'll write you afterwards to get the names of those two people." "I'll contact you once I hear from her."

**Send a thank-you note.** Within twenty-four hours, send a thank-you email, text, or note. This is not universally done, but it's something I insist on. You are classy if you do, and you are not classy if you don't. The reason to do it within twenty-four hours is that the longer you wait, the more likely perfectionistic tendencies will take over and you will delay further. A well-written email doesn't have to be long—just polite, correctly spelled, and capable of expressing appreciation.

Note: you should express your thanks even if you didn't get what you wanted. It's always appropriate to thank people for their time and their honesty.

---

### Manners

Manners are important. They are not antique or especially hard to implement. They are a socially understood way of communicating mutual respect. Manners are especially crucial when you don't know a person very well; they have limited data to go on, so you want any data they do have to show you in a positive light.

Since not everyone has been taught this in the same way, here is a short review:

1. **Proofread your communications.** When you reach out to people, proofread your messages to make sure you have no typos. If you're not good at proofreading, ask someone to check your messages before you send them.

2. **Don't be late.** If you are going to be late, even two minutes, message them with that information. This is especially important the first time you meet someone. I once had a coaching client who was the COO at a major media company. I was more than fifteen minutes late to our first appointment (there was traffic, a slow security line, etc., but let's face it, I didn't leave early enough). Epic fail. I acknowledged my mistake, apologized profusely, explained how I would never let it happen again, but I knew in that moment this engagement was not going to work. It didn't.

3. **Mute and stow your electronics.** You're either paying attention to the other person or to your phone, not both. Do not hold your phone in your hand, don't put it on the table in front of you, and don't leave it in an open position in a bag thinking that you can consult it without detection. If your phone rings or goes off during the conversation, reach over to turn it off *without looking at what the message is.* If you need to be available for some type of call, explain that at the beginning of the meeting. "I might get a call from my kid's school, so I'm leaving this on." Never walk into any meeting with headphones or earbuds in your ears.

4. **Be deliberate about how you dress.** I advise you to be equal or slightly better dressed than your counterpart. If it's a jeans and t-shirt culture, wear clean jeans and a nice t-shirt. If they

wear a suit, you wear a suit. Either way, you're showing that you are preparing with intention, not just rolling out of bed.

5. **Match their standing and sitting.** If they are standing when you come in, don't sit down until they do. If someone comes in the office and they stand up, then you stand up as well. (There is an exemption to women who are wearing dresses and shoes that may make it difficult to quickly rearrange themselves. It's okay to stay seated.)

6. **Send a thank-you note.** It shows you're a respectful person even after you've gotten (or not gotten) what you wanted.

## TWENTY-MINUTES-A-DAY EXERCISES

- **Exercise 1: Evaluate your balance of talking versus listening.** Ask someone who knows you well: In a conversation, what percentage of time do I speak vis-à-vis the other person? Take to heart their answer. If you are talking 50 percent of the time or more, try to push this down to 25 percent in your next few conversations. If you are at 25 percent talking or lower, try to push this up to 40 to 50 percent in your next few conversations. (At the same time, be mindful of your audience. If the other person really wants to be silent, you can speak more. Just don't talk as a default behavior.)

- **Exercise 2: Engineer a coincidence.** Plan an upcoming conversation with a weak tie. Write down your stated goal (e.g., "reconnect with old friend," "explore business possibilities," "learn about board service"). Then review the following prompts and see which ones grab you. Jot down your answers to the ones that interest you, and take a moment to wonder how the other person might respond to the same prompts:

  — Where you were born and grew up; cities you've lived in

  — Your family members; their interests

— Hobbies or special interests

— Communities or groups you're part of

— TV or other entertainment you love or are currently bingeing

— Countries you've visited

— Something you learned from a mentor, parent, or boss

— A challenge you've taken on

— Something that scares you right now

Consider introducing one or more of these into the conversation at the right moment or offering the prompt to the other person. The idea is to be open to the conversation moving in unexpected directions. After you have your meeting, reflect on whether it made a difference to think beyond your specific agenda.

- **Exercise 3: Propose an agenda.** Write out how you're going to kick off your next check-in session with your boss. "Thank you for taking this time to today. It's always useful to get your input. I thought we could start by X, then talk about Y. How does that sound?"

# CHAPTER 7
## How to Talk About Yourself Without Being Gross

One of my favorite shows to cringe-watch is the Netflix hit, *Emily in Paris*. The protagonist, Emily, is a twentysomething American woman from Chicago who willy-nilly finds herself in Paris. Emily has numerous entanglements with handsome, brooding locals, but the show really centers on her career and her attempts to get ahead. It's a show about careers disguised as a show about romance and culture.

I'm not just a consumer of light entertainment and wannabe Parisian; I'm also a professional in the careers space, so I watch this show with a critical eye. From a coaching perspective, *Emily in Paris* is a vivid depiction of someone with a lot of positive energy who manages constantly to get in her own way.

Emily is gung ho, confident, and positive. She brims with can-do spirit. She never wants to miss an opportunity, even if it means pitching deals while double-fisting plates of canapés and glasses of champagne. She illustrates the phrase I heard as a kid: "American" ends in "I Can."

Since "French" *doesn't* end in "I Can," things don't work out the way she wants. She misses cultural cues and makes faux pas after faux pas. Despite setting goals like nobody's business, Emily constantly makes errors of judgment. She can't figure out the vibe at French family brunches, and she occasionally offends clients. Her friends find her adorably naive, and her boss finds her annoyingly naive. The colleagues she is seeking to impress alternately ignore her and outfox her. Emily has so much energy, but she hits the gas pedal and the brake pedal at the same time, without ever understanding why she's not moving forward. "Why isn't this working?" you can imagine her saying. "I'm trying so hard!" And *that* is why she has my sympathy.

Even as I watch half-covering my eyes, I want her to succeed. I actually want to be more like Emily myself. She is confident—she starts off with forty-seven Instagram followers but calls herself a social media expert? Why not? You go, Emily! She has good intentions. She's a go-getter who believes in win-win outcomes. She's straightforward. She doesn't hide what she wants from her career, she doesn't minimize herself, and she doesn't wait for permission to become who she wants to be. She's tiny and walks on precarious heels, but she doesn't hesitate to take up space. She constantly talks about herself and her ideas. Sometimes her words have their intended effect, many times they don't, but she never goes silent.

To fully access your invisible network, you need to talk about yourself, your interests, your desires, your value. How to do so is not obvious, and even when you know the key principles, it takes a lot of practice. Communication isn't simply about your messages. It's also about how your audience takes in what you are saying, how you stimulate their thinking, how you make it easy for them to understand you and help you.

There are social codes behind all communication. People are reacting to you as a person as well as to your ideas. When we hesitate, it's usually because we're afraid of falling on the wrong side of decorum. We don't want a Sylvie staring at us in barely disguised contempt. But being silent or staying small is no solution.

Talking about yourself is an art. There is a ton of nuance. But guess what? It's learnable. You can do it, and you can steadily improve your performance.

## Your Voice, Your Responsibility

In the United States, the most common first question is, "What do you do?" You're supposed to have an answer to this question, which really means, "Tell me about yourself. Tell me what I need to know."

This creates a responsibility, and even a burden. We expect you to make the first move. If you fail to do so, the view is, well, you had your chance.

To achieve your potential, you need to talk about yourself. You need to do it *well*. Not perfectly, but competently. And you need to do in a way that's not gross, not so much because other people will be repelled, but because if you feel gross about it, you aren't going to do it.

## No One Else Can Do Your Job

You are the primary advocate for your own career. You care more about it than anyone else, and you know more about it than anyone else. If you don't talk about your capabilities, interests, and goals, no one will.

The way you advocate is through conversations and various types of writing. Words, tone, and energy are what connect your capabilities, interests, and ambitions to people and opportunities. There is no magical computer or app that will implant an awareness of your capabilities into someone else's head. Given that you are taking the initiative to set up conversations that will hopefully establish and deepen relationships, you need to also do the work of explaining what they should know about you. Other people might intervene on your behalf, but you need to arm them with the right messages.

Talking about yourself includes an element of self-promotion—actively sharing with the world the positive things you can do and the things you are interested in. Here are some specific reasons.

## Decisions About (or Relevant to) Your Career Are Made in Rooms You Are Not In

In the professional world, people will be evaluating you all the time. They'll be deciding who to interview, who to hire, and what salary to offer. They'll be parceling out assignments and looking at workload distribution. They'll be assessing your performance formally and informally. They'll be deciding on promotions, performance improvement plans, and exits. They will have some good data, possibly some bad data, and *a lot* of assumptions—about your talents, interests, ambitions, plans, and about the part of you that never shows up at work. They have assumptions because that's the only way they—or anyone, including you—can get through life.

In many cases, they will have no way to get additional information if you don't tell them, either because you're the only one who knows about this relevant information or it never occurs to them to ask.

### Other People Are Not Mind Readers

Don't rely on other people to read your mind. If you want something specific for your birthday, tell your partner. Don't expect them to guess and then punish them when they don't. Guessing correctly is not a sign that they truly care for you. Similarly, don't presume that a "good" networking conversation or negotiation is one where the other person guesses exactly what you need.

Do you want a promotion? Ask for a promotion. Are you happy? Say you're happy. Do you want to join the DEI team? Say you want to.

### People Rarely Know How to Represent You If You Don't Tell Them

There are many people in your life who would be happy to help you. This includes talking you up, putting in a word, giving additional details, and so on. It is far easier for them to do a good job if you equip them with the right information.

A few years ago, I had lunch with a contact of mine at an advertising firm. I had done successful coaching engagements there, and I liked the firm's scrappy energy. I was eager to do more. My contact, Clement, was happy to help. He shared some of their new plans.

"We're bringing in someone to do a networking workshop for new managers," he gushed. "I'm excited we're finally doing this kind of thing."

*Uh, hello?* I thought. *I do networking workshops. I can do amazing networking workshops.* But Clement and his colleagues knew me through coaching and actually had no idea of these other capabilities. It was my job to tell them, and I had already missed that particular train.

Even people who know you well may only see one side of you or have an outdated draft of your priorities.

## Intermediaries Can Help a Lot—Especially If They Are Informed

We focus a lot on end users—trying to find that one person who can help us. But intermediaries play a huge role in careers, in business development, and in success generally. An intermediary is anyone who might mention you to a third party. It could be a colleague, a neighbor, a classmate, a personal trainer, a client, and so on.

I have had many caregivers for my kids over the years, and I realized that most of them originated with one person named Benjamin, whom I originally met twenty years ago when we had the same personal trainer at our gym. Benjamin and I regard each other well and don't live far away from one another, but we have probably had three conversations in ten years.

I happened to speak to him just before my kids were born. I had called a couple of agencies to find a night nurse for my kids' early weeks. Benjamin emailed me, "I can get the name of the person my friends use if you'd like," and mentioned a gay couple he knew.

"Um, sure," I said, wondering if I really wanted to follow this up. I already had a lot of preparing-for-babies chores on my list.

I did follow up, and thank goodness I did. I met Precious, a very experienced Jamaican baby nurse who specialized in twins and multiples. She came to work an hour after I'd arrived from South Dakota with my twelve-day-old sons and went to work. Through her I met many other loving, competent Jamaican caregivers: her daughter, Denise, as well as Ina and Sharon. Sharon led to Sandra and Barbara.

I had another nanny, Maria, a Colombian woman who had originally been my cleaning lady but conveyed an interest in the job. She worked as full-time nanny for two years. And then I realized that it had been Benjamin who was the source of that connection, too: Maria was a friend of his cleaning lady, Melba.

I also hosted an au pair for a couple of years. Paula was also from Colombia. But the reason I found her was that I had signed up through an agency called Cultural Care au Pair, which I had done because I was talking with a client who was also the mom of twins, and she had hosted an au pair from that agency for a year.

Intermediaries will help you if they understand what you need.

Intermediaries tend to have their biggest impact over time—when you first talk to an intermediary, they may have no information or connections to offer. But a week, month, or year later, they may be in a situation where they can help you.

## Our Mixed Cultural Message About Self-Promotion

One of the challenges of talking about yourself is that there don't seem to be all that many examples of people who do this well, whereas there are plenty of examples of people who do it poorly. In addition, our culture gives mixed messages. We Americans are known as people who have no problem going on about ourselves. We have a reputation for being smiley and upbeat. We appreciate self-confidence. Yet at the same time, we don't like braggarts or self-absorbed people.

It's hard to get this self-promotion thing right.

There are two types of fails when it comes to talking about yourself:

- Too strong
- Too weak

The too strong category consists of people who are confident, assertive, and proactive, but too much so. Emily falls in this category, and she is by no means an extreme example. Most networking books I have read were written by people who make me a little uncomfortable. Their "Me Me Me energy" is loud and off-putting. I read their advice, and I think, "Check, please!"

The other category is people who hesitate to talk about themselves, don't know what to say, or do it in weak and ineffectual ways. You have a conversation with them, and you think, "Huh?" They might be nice, but your eyes might glaze over when they speak.

A friend of mine observed a meeting of a leadership program for young government staffers. They were mostly first-generation professionals who had won places in a very selective program. My friend, who is also first generation, listened to their self-introductions, and was concerned on their behalf. They used only their first names, they giggled or mumbled while they were talking, and they gave very little information about their backgrounds or the interesting things they were doing. "I'm Sandra and, um, gosh these things are always so embarrassing, ha ha." This was a lost opportunity.

Weak communications aren't limited to people who may lack role models in the work force. I've had clients grimace when they practice their positioning statements—the basic elevator pitch they use when meeting people. A client who had won a Pulitzer Prize used to roll her eyes when she'd deliver her own introduction to me.

I'd put the relative standing of these two categories as 30/70. In my experience, a minority of people are in the overconfident category of ineffectiveness, and a majority of people are in the hesitating category of ineffectiveness. And holding back is not good.

## Why We Hold Back

There are valid reasons, or at least understandable fears, for not talking about yourself and what you want. If you hesitate, you're not alone.

### Anxiety About Imposing

A phrase my mom repeated many times in my childhood was, "Don't impose." Don't make someone make extra efforts for you, don't ask for favors, don't bother people. My mother is a proactive person who has never hesitated to stand up for herself—she was born in a house with a dirt floor, was the eleventh of twelve kids, was the first in her extended family to attend college, later earned a PhD, and, after my parents' divorce, raised my two sisters and me by herself. I learned assertiveness from her as well: by example she taught us how to march into the financial office to ask for more money, how to ask strangers for directions, and generally never to pre-reject ourselves from opportunities. The fact that she conveyed the imperative of not imposing on others shows how deep the thinking goes. "Don't impose" reflects a constant anxiety that we might slip over the line into inappropriate behavior and bug people.

### Fear of Getting Slapped Down

Australia and New Zealand have a unique phrase: "cutting down the tall poppy." This means that if you excel beyond your peers, you are easy to spot and will be whacked down. Excellence and ambition may be interpreted as an attack on the norm. Many cultures have a push toward conformity.

Not everyone is rewarded for assertiveness. Research shows that men interrupt and talk over women in meetings, mostly without being aware of it, yet dislike it when women interrupt or talk over them. People who are minorities may experience reproach when they speak up for themselves. Our cultural inheritance includes stereotypes: "angry" Black woman, "fiery" Latina, "deferential" Asian, "argumentative" Indian. You can be punished if others see you as the stereotype ("There she goes again"), and you can also be punished if you depart from the stereotype ("You're not acting the way I thought you would act").

## A Belief That Winging It Is More Authentic

Some people believe that winging it is more authentic than planning what you are going to say. They don't want to hamper their free spirits. Surely their counterpart will be more interested in their natural self than a scripted version. The trouble is, the winged version often isn't all that good.

Extroverts tend to suffer from this belief more than introverts. Extroverts are usually more comfortable chatting people up. In contrast, introverts feel less comfortable in new or unplanned conversations and are therefore more likely to prepare. They often end up sounding more coherent.

## Your Basic Positioning Statement

Everything starts with your core positioning statement. This is the first thing you say, *not the only thing you say.* Your positioning statement could be the first forty seconds of an hourlong meeting. Therefore, you don't need to put everything in. But it needs some intelligent design because this sets up everything that will come after it. You want to establish yourself as credible, pleasant to talk to, and someone who has some clarity about what you are trying to achieve. This applies to networking conversations of all kinds, not just those for job search.

Professional conversations often start with some version of:

- "Tell me about yourself."
- "So, what have you been up to?"
- "How can I help you?"

The meta meaning of these statements is, "Please start the conversation." You can use your judgment about how to start.

When you start a conversation, you want to communicate three things:

1. Who you are
2. What you're looking for
3. What you want to accomplish in this conversation

This can be either very light or more detailed. Let's look at some examples.

> Who I am · What I want
>
> "I'm a **sophomore in college,** and I'm interested in a **career in marketing**. I'd
>
> Seeking in this conversation
>
> like to get your ideas about which **courses I should be taking** to set myself up for a
>
> good entry-level position upon graduation."

> Who I am · Who I am
>
> "We are **moving to Dallas** for my wife's job. She works in finance, and **I'm an architect**.
>
> What I want · What I want
>
> We're trying to figure out **schools**, which means **figuring out where to rent or**
>
> Seeking in this conversation
>
> **buy**. Stella says that you know everything about Dallas so **I'd love some pointers**."

> Who I am
>
> "I've had my **head down for the past ten years to try to make partner,** and,
>
> What I want
>
> hooray, I just made it! I'm a political junkie and one day would like to **run for public**
>
> Seeking in this conversation
>
> **office**. I know you're involved in party politics, and **I'd love to talk about how I**
>
> **could plant some early seeds**, given that I'll be working intense hours for many
>
> years to come."

> Who I am
>
> "**I'm Lupe Vasconcellos. I graduated two years ago from ASU and I'm cur-**
>
> **rently working in Senator Robinson's office. I'm thrilled to be part of this**
>
> What I want
>
> **emerging leaders program**, and I **look forward to learning from each of you**

$\boxed{\text{Seeking in this conversation}}$

*in the next year.* **Today I'm just glad to meet everyone.** *I love to make sweet*

$\boxed{\text{Who I am}}$ $\boxed{\text{What I want}}$

*Christmas tamales,* so **you're all invited to my place in December."**


$\boxed{\text{Who I am}}$

**"I'm June Davis. I recently came into the role of managing sales in the**

**Southeast region after running our Florida division for the past five years.**

$\boxed{\text{What I want}}$

*I like to establish a personal connection with each of our clients.* We will have

$\boxed{\text{Seeking in this conversation}}$

plenty of meetings to talk business, but **for this first call I'd like for us to get to**

**know each other better.** How does that sound?"


In general, people spend far too much time going into details about their backgrounds—their entire career trajectory, their accomplishments, their questions, and their feelings. Part of the problem is that we feel we must justify why we are in this conversation. But the more you say, the more you are likely to turn off your listener. I hear a lot of people getting lost in their own words. Sometimes they'll even look up with a puzzled expression, as if unclear how their thoughts have gotten to this point and wondering if they should keep talking.


## Additional Tips

Getting this right comes from practice. Don't practice to make perfect; practice to make it good enough.

Here are some additional tips to help enliven your positioning statements.


### 1. Experiment with Your "Who I Am" Anchors

Who am I? The first thing that comes to mind may not be the most relevant or interesting. You can express who you are in different ways:

| Job | • "I'm a teacher trainer for the district. I lead formal programs and serve as an ad hoc coach for principals." |
|---|---|
| Career Trajectory | • "I've spent fifteen years working in youth-oriented social service agencies in New York. I started on the social work side and, for the past four years, have been in charge of operations for a large settlement house." |
| Personal Brand | • "Usually I'm representing the spouse who has supported the career of the wealthier partner, and is now at risk of getting screwed. I make sure they don't." |
| Current Projects | • "My company started a program to improve preparation for tech careers at the high school level, and I'm in charge of building the partner network." |
| Skills | • "I work with lots of big egos, and I'm good at managing them to get positive results." |
| Interests | • "I have a passion for reducing the amount of plastic in the oceans. I'm involved in two organizations fighting this, and I regularly volunteer for beach clean-ups." |
| Alternate Identity | • "I'm a loving, involved dad who happens to earn his living as an executive coach." |

## 2. Articulate Your Goals, Interests, and Directions for Exploration

What are you trying to accomplish? You might be clear about your goal or you have a hypothesis of what your goal might be.

- "I want to figure out when I can say no or push back on assignments."
- "I just came over from another company and want to understand the culture here."
- "I want to learn how to use this job as a platform to discover more about blockchain."

### 3. Feel Free to Start with Your Interests, Not Your Background

You don't have to start with an overview of your background. It's fine to kick off with what you're interested in.

- "I'm studying up on blockchain, and I can't get enough of this. By way of background, I spent six years as a programmer in a series of tech start-ups."

Starting with your interests can put you in a better, more energetic space and lessen the chance you'll get lost in detail.

### 4. Figure Out What You Want from This Conversation

Sometimes you'll know; sometimes you'll need to use your best guess. If you don't know, ask a friend: What should I be trying to accomplish in this conversation?

- "I'm trying to decide if I should stay with the bank during this crisis and possibly get a battlefield promotion, or if I should make a jump now."
- "I'm wondering if joining this internal committee will get me more exposure, or if it's considered 'women's work' and will not count for anything meaningful."
- "I'm wondering what you've found effective in dealing with our boss."

You also want to *be able to define where you are in the process*—beginning, middle, or approaching the end of the tunnel.

- "I've just started these conversations. I'm doing my homework before making any big asks."
- "I've been in this field for several years but am taking a few steps back to see what has changed."
- "I'm going to make a decision in the next two weeks. I can tell you how I'm leaning, and I'd love a reality check."

Identifying where you are in the process helps people know how to help you. This will also allow you to graciously put off offers of help if they are coming at the wrong time or in a form you can't use.

## TWENTY-MINUTES-A-DAY EXERCISES

- **Exercise 1: Emily in Paris.** Watch an episode of *Emily in Paris*. Identify what she's doing well and how she gets in her own way. Extra credit if you watch and discuss with a friend.
- **Exercise 2: Whom do you need to update?**

  1. Make a list of five people who are important to you professionally.
  2. For each of these, evaluate, "How up to date are they on my interests and goals?" Use a 1 to 5 scale, where 5 is "on top of it" and 1 is "no clue."
  3. Pick one person to catch up with and let them know what's currently going on with you.

- **Exercise 3: Competency identification.**

  1. Brainstorm your competencies (all the things you know how to do). If you're not sure what your competencies are, ask yourself, "If I had to hire someone to live my life, what skills, knowledge, or traits would they need to have?
  2. Reduce this list to four key competencies. These may or may not be the most important ones, but they feel relevant to you.
  3. Put these on a Post-it in a prominent place.

# CHAPTER 8
# Vulnerability Is Strength

F or several years I gave presentations at MBA programs alongside my colleague Rebecca. A consistent crowd pleaser was a workshop called "Creating a Career Marketing Plan." You might think that MBA students would already be good at this kind of thing, but they needed help.

Most of these schools were selective, and their students were proud of themselves for getting in. They were ambitious and imagined, usually correctly, that great things were ahead for them. Rebecca and I were selected because we could meet this type of elite positioning head on. We had both graduated from Stanford Business School, had coached people at companies the students were seeking to enter, and knew insider-y lingo (e.g., bulge bracket, family office, search fund). Rebecca had worked at Goldman Sachs, which, along with McKinsey, was the ultimate "made it" credential, at least for MBA students in their twenties. This credibility was important because MBA students would dismiss in two minutes anyone who they thought wasn't at their level or they felt was wasting their extremely important time.

To be a good presenter, you need to tell stories. Concepts are straightforward; it's the stories that bring things to life. We tried out a lot of stories taken from client work and our own lives. Some resonated deeply, and others landed flat.

Here's what I learned: Audiences were not much interested in hearing about our successes, even though we had been hired partly because of them. MBA students demanded that level of accomplishment, yet they were not actually interested in it. Hearing about speakers' wins left them feeling distanced. They hadn't gotten into Stanford, and many of them would never get a serious interview at Goldman Sachs.

On the other hand, when we spoke honestly about our own setbacks, frustrations, and mistakes, they were riveted. They found these stories gripping. If I talked about getting laid off from a hedge fund, running a start-up that failed, or being unemployed for a year, they were interested in how I handled this. If Rebecca talked about working for a global media company but hating every minute of it, they wondered how she got herself out of that situation. If we spoke about a client who never had a successful final round interview but then changed her preparation approach and got the offer, they took notes. Everyone has setbacks, and the MBA student audiences were interested in how we dealt with those, all the more because they respected us.

## Beyond the Humble Brag

Consider the difference:

"I worked really hard and got into private equity."
"I worked hard, got into private equity, and then discovered I didn't like the actual work."

Or

"I went to the event, followed a strategy, and came out with two great
    contacts."
"I went to the event, felt awkward, and left without talking to anyone
    new."

Who would you rather speak to? The first lines are respectable but life-
less. The second ones are intriguing: Hmm, I could imagine that happening
to me. I wonder what I would do.

The listener is processing the setback yet also knows that this wasn't
the end of the road. You're here talking to me. You look professional to me.
Something else happened to get you here. I want to know what you learned.
And often: you must be a pretty strong person to keep going and then share
this with me.

Showing vulnerability is not humble bragging. And it's not false mod-
esty deployed to be socially accepted. It's authentically sharing doubts, setbacks, disappointments, uncertainties, and all the things that make us less
perfect but more human.

Vulnerability is strength. Showing vulnerability helps you make deeper,
better connections. Be more vulnerable, and make it possible for others to
be vulnerable with you.

## Vulnerability Deepens Relationships

Humans are social animals. We are hungry for real human connections and
seek ways to make those happen.

Life is complicated, and at any moment, most of us are experiencing
some combination of being confident and thinking *WTF?* We're all trying
to figure it out. So when you meet someone who seems *real*, it's a special
experience. It's a relief to take off the mask.

There are valid reasons for *not* showing vulnerability. The other person might respond negatively. Or they might not respond at all. You can't control the outcome. Think of every time in your life when you liked someone—and showed it—and they didn't like you back.

Vulnerability in a business setting is complicated because part of being businesslike is focusing on the agenda at hand. The way we dress, the way we talk, the way we start meetings and conversations—these are all signals that we are going to conform to a certain way of doing things for the purpose of aligning and getting things done. It's not clear where the line is between what will be accepted in the workplace and what won't. How much of your real self can you let out? How much of your real self should you let out?

You are taking a risk by showing more vulnerability in professional settings. It's worthwhile, and the rewards are great, but it is a risk. Therefore, let's take a risk-managed approach.

In their book, *Connect: Building Exceptional Relationships with Family, Friends, and Colleagues*, David Bradford and Carole Robin explain that vulnerability in relationships relates in part to our position in three zones of being—the Zone of Comfort, the Zone of Danger, and the Zone of Learning:

- The Zone of Comfort is where you don't have to think twice before saying or doing something.
- The Zone of Danger is when saying or doing something is too scary or risky for you.
- The Zone of Learning is where you are willing to face discomfort and you take a minor risk to see what happens.

You get to the Zone of Learning by taking what they call "15 percent risks." When you take a 15 percent risk, you are stretching yourself to try something out of your comfort zone but not doing something that will make you feel debilitated if the result doesn't hit the mark.

To arrive at your Zone of Learning, think of something scary, and then do something less scary. Or, alternately, think of something easy, and then do something harder. Consider these examples:

| Situation | Too Easy (Zone of Comfort) | Too Scary (Zone of Danger) | 15 Percent Risk (Zone of Learning) |
|---|---|---|---|
| You want to talk to your imposing boss about your career. | You say hello to your boss at a company function and say your job has started off well. | You ask your boss for a half-hour meeting to share your longer-term career goals. | You and a colleague jointly invite your boss to lunch in the coming weeks. |
| You're upset about fertility problems, and colleagues are picking up on your distress. | You tell a colleague you've been going through some stuff. | You tell a colleague you have had two miscarriages. | You tell your colleague you want to become a parent, but the process has been hard. |
| You're curious how someone who has his own coaching business has managed the trade-off between money and fulfillment. | You say you'd like to learn more about his career. | You ask how he could leave a sweet job at a top-tier law firm to operate in the wilds of self-employment. | You observe, "You've made some career changes that other people might find hard," and say you'd love to learn how he did it. |
| Your buddy seems upset about something. | You wait to see if he brings anything up. | You say, "It's clear you're upset about something. Tell me what's going on. Maybe I can help." | You say, "How about we go shoot some hoops?" |

The idea is to get to the Zone of Learning, where you are stretching yourself (and possibly the other person) but not taking on a bigger risk than you can handle. You stretch by taking 15 percent risks. Be 15 percent more assertive. Be 15 percent more honest. Be 15 percent more uncomfortable. Things may go well, or the other person may not engage, or they may have a negative reaction—but it won't be so negative that you can't recover. Take a baby step in the relationship—but take a step, nonetheless.

## How to Introduce Vulnerability

When you introduce vulnerability to a conversation or relationship, you are not just opening yourself up. You're inviting the other person to do the same. You're sharing of yourself, but you're also saying, "Hey, let's try this out."

There are five practical ways you can do this:

1. Mix personal and professional topics.
2. Work toward next-level listening.
3. Acknowledge your setbacks, disappointments, and failures.
4. Be open about uncertainty and lack of resolution.
5. Hold something painful or hard for the other person.

### 1. Mix Personal and Professional Topics

In general we regard the professional realm as a place where we are businesslike and focused on business matters. We have agendas, decks, and bullet points. We center on competence: I can do this, I bring this value, you can rely on me for that, here are the next steps. Yet we are still human beings.

A simple way to leaven this all-work focus is to start sharing details about your personal life. This can include:

| Your family | • "I keep a list of funny things my sons say. Today it was, 'remembery.' Like, 'Daddy, you have a bad remembery.'" |
|---|---|
| What you do outside of work | • "I have a board meeting tonight, but I will email you my comments afterwards. I think you remember this organization—it partners with high-needs high schools in East St. Louis." |
| The weather | • "Does anyone ever get used to how cold it is in San Francisco in the summer?" |
| Upcoming plans and goals | • "We're going to LEGOLAND this weekend. My husband likes it because everything is in bright primary colors, so the photos all come out great." |
| Shows you're bingeing and books you're reading | • "The whole time I was bingeing *Never Have I Ever* on Netflix I was texting my best Indian girlfriends. It was like seeing my high school psyche on television." |
| The things that make you tick: your joys and irritations, your achievements and setbacks, what brings out your best, and what triggers your worst | • "I have a thing about loud noises. I always carry a bag of earplugs in my purse. If you need some, let me know."<br>• "I get a kick helping people carry baby strollers up the subway stairs. It's probably one of my greatest pleasures in life."<br>• "Apparently I have kind of a crabby resting facial expression. I think I'm just being calm and pensive, and then other people are like, 'Dude, lighten up.'"<br>• "I come in half an hour early to have my alone time. If I get to have my coffee in solitude, I can be amazing for the rest of the day." |
| Past Setbacks | • "I've been fired before. They were all, 'We don't think this is a fit,' and I was all, 'You're totally right.'" |

When you share personal details, other people take the cue to do the same. You naturally find common interests and deeper emotional connections.

## 2. Work Toward Next-Level Listening

Most people think they are good listeners already. But you can get better. In deep listening, you are turning the spotlight on the other person and keeping your attention on them, not on yourself.

There is a continuum of listening, ranging from non-listening to deep listening.

1.  **Non-listening.** This is when you are pretending to listen but are distracted or doing something else. Recall every bad conference call you've participated in.
2.  **Semi-listening.** This is when you are listening enough to identify when you can break in with your own thoughts, opinions, or answers. Typically, you are waiting for your chance to say your piece.
3.  **Literal listening.** You're hearing the words coming out of someone else's mouth and making sense of them. You are contemplating what is being said. You are not tuning into the nonliteral elements, such as nonverbal signals.
4.  **Fuller listening.** This is hearing the substance of their words and also taking in cues like body language, timbre, emotion. You notice when their expression doesn't match their words, and you track energy.
5.  **Deep listening.** This is a combination of number four, plus something coaches call "standing on the balcony." Imagine that normal conversation and interactions take place on the dance floor, but periodically you can climb up the stairs to a balcony for a different view of what's happening. You're observing the dynamic rather than being caught up in it. You're noticing what's being said and what's not being said.

The most powerful listening tool is active listening. Active listening is the practice of reflecting back or summarizing what the other person has said, asking them for confirmation, and then possibly asking another question that keeps them talking and exploring.

**Speaker:** "We went through a reorg, and I'm the one who had to communicate the reduction in force to everyone. I had twenty-eight individual meetings telling people the company was letting them go. I barely slept for two months."

**Listener:** "So your company went through a reorg, and you were the one charged with termination meetings. It sounds like it was incredibly stressful. Is that right?"

**Speaker:** "Exactly. I don't want to ever go through that again."

**Listener:** "How did you manage the stress?"

When we actively listen, we are curious. We're trying to understand things from the point of view of the other person. Great listening is inherently nonjudgmental. This is important because vulnerability looks for a safe space to hang out in. We hesitate to be vulnerable partly because we are afraid of the potential reaction—will I be embarrassed, misunderstood, or shamed? Showing you are a good listener makes it easier for people to share.

## 3. Acknowledge Your Setbacks, Disappointments, and Failures

Other people's success is a boring topic. People who are presented as successful—either by themselves or others—have a shiny quality. There's nothing to grab onto. You might learn something from them, but do you really connect with them? In contrast, when you know someone has had dark days, you are more likely to see them as a real person who might understand your own mix of experiences.

Introducing vulnerability is not exactly the same as sharing every negative thing you are experiencing. Every extended family has someone who is a master of getting attention for their unique condition without ever doing much to change it.

What I mean in terms of introducing vulnerability in professional settings is providing a balanced view of your life as it actually is—this isn't the glossed-up, shiny version, and it's not the "my life sucks" version. When you talk about yourself and admit vulnerability, you are including some things from the not-so-positive column as well as the positive one.

You can share your setbacks in a way that is factual, not performative, by just stating the things that happened:

- "I got laid off."
- "The company went bankrupt."
- "My kid's having some problems at school."
- "We didn't get the deal."
- "The relationship didn't work out."

When people hear statements like these, they feel sympathy, and they probably also wonder how they would deal with the same situation. Many people will respond with compassion, respect, and appropriate curiosity—which means trying to sense what *you* want to talk about, not what they personally are curious about.[1]

## 4. Be Open About Uncertainty and Lack of Resolution

Much of the time when you are connecting with other people you won't have things all wrapped up. There will be open questions, loose ends, uncertainties. Everyone is familiar with the uncertainties of life, so when you can communicate them coherently, you demonstrate vulnerability and grounded-ness.

---

1. This type of compassionate response may include short statements or questions, followed by pauses that invite the other person to continue, if they want to. "I'm sorry" (pause). "How are you feeling?" (pause). "What happened?" (pause).

Here are some examples of how you can be open about uncertainty:

- "The offer with the new company is really exciting, but I just started a new role here and like working with my boss. So I'm not sure what I'm going to do."
- "I'm not especially happy with how things are in my relationship, but I'm also not ready to leave."
- "We've tried a lot of activities for our son. Soccer, basketball, tae kwon do, swimming, dance. He didn't like any of them. He is a very active child, so I'm still searching around for something that might stick with him. It's a bit of a mystery."
- "We're seeing another specialist to get her opinion, and then we'll assess our options. It's not an easy time, but we're trying keep our spirits up."

There's a predisposition in our culture toward "Get it done!" and "Tell me the answer!" Yet we know what life is like. It doesn't fit in neat compartments. Uncertainty and irresolution are deeply cognizable on a human level.

## 5. Hold Something Painful or Hard for the Other Person

Accepting vulnerability from others doesn't mean trying to fix anything. It means being there with them. You're holding a space, not solving a problem.

To do this well, you have to manage your own anxiety and discomfort.

When someone shares a vulnerability—a hard moment, a sad experience, a trembling uncertainty—the immediate impulse of many people is to try to *soothe* them: to make them feel better, to lessen the bad feeling, to share some happiness.

There is an element of helping here but also an element of self-protection. It's not easy to be around someone else's pain. If you use soothing words, are you soothing the other person? Or are you protecting yourself from discomfort, or anxiety, or guilt?

If someone says, "I feel like no one values me here" and your response is, "I'm sorry you feel that way; we totally value you," you are short-circuiting their feeling. You are not actually allowing the person to be vulnerable, and you are not being vulnerable yourself. You are getting yourself off the hook, and you're hoping that by doing so the person's negative feeling goes away.

People deal with many, many things that are beyond your quick fixes:

| | |
|---|---|
| Frustrations in achieving a goal | • I was rejected for the third time from medical school. |
| Job or career problems | • I've been soldiering away for three years, and she waltzed in here six months ago and just got the promotion I deserved. |
| Relationship problems | • He refuses to talk about anything. He won't even consider going to a couple's counselor. |
| Issues or worries about children or family | • I'm worried that my son's speech is delayed. I can't stand when the teacher talks to me with this *concern* in her voice. |
| Health problems | • I'm overweight. I've always been heavy, but now I'm prediabetic. |
| Financial problems | • We're under water with our mortgage. |
| Just a bad day (or month, or year) | • Everything has gone wrong at work this week. And this morning our pipes burst. |

If someone shares these with you, they are expressing vulnerability. If they want help or your advice, they will probably ask you directly. If they don't ask, it's probably not your job to offer it. Your job is to just be with them and show that you hear them.

- "I'm sorry that happened."
- "That sucks."
- "That's tough."
- "You're going through a lot."

An experienced parent gave me some advice just before my kids were born. He said, "When your kids are sharing something hard, don't overtalk. Just shut up. Just listen and say, 'Oh.' At the most say, 'That's really hard.'"

When my children have tough days, the cure isn't my saying something reassuring to them. The cure is my being with them. The same is true of adults. When someone shows vulnerability, your first and foremost task is just to be with them. Time is love. So is presence.

## TWENTY-MINUTES-A-DAY EXERCISES

- **Exercise 1: Open people.** Make a list of three people who seem comfortable talking about their vulnerabilities and connect with one of those people. This is a "social contagion" type of activity—you don't need to plan to talk about any specific vulnerability; you just want to spend time with people who do this naturally.
- **Exercise 2: Open questions.** Write three big (doubt-related) questions you're trying to answer in your life. Some possible prompts: "I'm not sure if . . . ," "I'm still working through whether . . . ," or "An area where I have both hopes and doubts is . . ."
- **Exercise 3: Tell me more.** Get better at active listening by saying, "Tell me more." In active listening you can still talk, but your purpose is to keep the spotlight on the other person. A good way is to use variations of the phrase, "Tell me more."
  — "That's cool. Tell me more."
  — "Say more about that."
  — "That sounds hard. What happened then?"
  — "What else do you have planned?"

# CHAPTER 9
# Managing Your Weak Tie Network

One of my Facebook friends is Ana, who is a business owner living in Hawaii. Ana lived down the street from me in Anaheim, California, when I was in junior high and high school. We didn't know each other well but were in adjacent social circles. My recollection is that she was in the band and also an athlete, which was not a mixture commonly seen at the time. We had a couple of classes together. I was in a play with her sister. A normal high school kind of acquaintanceship.

Several decades later, Ana and I are reconnected on Facebook. We have occasionally commented on each other's posts, and she read my book, *The Creative Lawyer*, and wrote a nice Amazon review for it. She wondered if I was going to attend our high school's reunion and was disappointed that I was not going to. We are closer now, without any actual in-person contact, than we ever were growing up.

In previous eras, Ana and I would not have maintained contact. We would not have come across one another, and it would have been difficult for either of us to find out what the other was up to. But social media makes it easy—and not just Facebook: LinkedIn, Twitter, and Instagram all make it easy to connect with weak ties. My invisible network is far vaster than it could have been in prior generations. That's a wonder, and it's also a complication. I can benefit from this, but I also have to keep track of it. I have more things in my head.

It's not just that I have more connections because of social media. I have collected more connections in the course of living than I could have in earlier times. I have moved around a lot in my life. I've lived in Southern and Northern California, New York, Massachusetts, Washington, D.C., India, and Taiwan. In every one of those places, I got to know people.

I've also moved from one career to another, several times. I met people when I was in college and grad school, when working in the Foreign Service, in management consulting, as a lawyer in a big firm and a hedge fund, during my phase with a start-up, and as a coach for twenty years.

When I became a dad, I entered a new type of social network. Parents have lots in common with other parents, and kids' activities have a way of driving you into the proximity of other parents.[1]

Most books on networking focus on how you expand your number of contacts, but in this case, we need to ask: What are you to do with all the people who are already there? How are you supposed to manage all of this? And should you?

The answer is yes, you should manage this. And you don't have to go crazy doing so. Let's talk about categories, methods, and systems for managing your invisible network.

In chapter three, I made the point that the size and value of your network grows over time. This is an opportunity, but also a challenge: Because your contacts are becoming more successful, there is a greater opportunity

---

1. Granted, I've been working for more than thirty years, I move more than most people, and I'm in a client service business where I regularly meet new people. But even a few years into my career, I had already come across a lot of people.

cost for not keeping in touch. If you don't keep up with your network, it's like not bothering to apply for a scholarship that you could probably easily win.

And yet, you can't keep up with everyone, or in the same manner, because you don't have time. The built-in conundrum is that the more relationships you have, the less time you can spend with each one. You might become a bit more efficient, but you can't change the iron law of time.

You need some type of system to follow—a set of habits and tools so that you aren't making things up as you go along. Fortunately there are a variety of approaches you can take to manage your weak tie network.

## Ways You Can Connect

There's an assumption that reaching out to people means *getting together*. That's one outcome, but it's not the only one. There are a variety of ways you can connect with people in meaningful ways.

Let's look at these by level of investment and intensity—greater to lesser. Keep in mind that what something costs someone else might be different from what it costs you.

**Getting together in person—higher investment.** There's no substitute for being with someone. Live interaction is less programmed. You experience the full humanity of the other person, not just a screenshot. Showing up to see the person live also demonstrates the investment you're making. You can have a meeting, have lunch or dinner, or go to an event.

**Getting together in person—lower investment.** Not every in-person meeting requires you to go to Soho or fly to Florida. You can get coffee with someone at your job. You can have a quick drink after work. You can take a short walk at lunch. You can agree to meet each other during a break at a professional event or sit next to one another during a presentation.

**Attending group events.** One of the purposes of professional gatherings is to make it easy for people to connect. The organizers have done your legwork for you. You can take part in an industry association, join a professional organization, take part in an employee resource group (ERG), join others in a volunteer effort, or serve on a nonprofit board. You can join a golf club, if that's your thing.

**Phone or video calls.** The pandemic revealed how we can connect meaningfully with people and get stuff done without being in the same place. (It also showed the limits of these, but that's another story.) These are far easier to schedule than an in-person meeting because no one needs to go anywhere. You can easily say, "Let's have a Zoom catch-up" instead of "Let's get a drink."

**Email.** The above categories are all synchronous. You can also have asynchronous connections—where you don't have to be communicating at the same time. Email is a prime example. You send a message with some context and questions, and the other person can respond. Many people prefer this because it takes less time, they can do it when they want, and there is less immediate pressure to respond to whatever you are asking. It can feel safer to people. There is no requirement that you rush a response.

**Slack and other instant messaging platforms** are a synchronous version of email. You are typing but having a live, or reasonably continuous, conversation.

You can do the same thing with oral communication using voice memos on platforms like WhatsApp. A few years ago, I was in Colombia. I'm into public transportation, so I was keen to try out the aerial gondola system (Metrocable) that operates over the hillsides of Medellín. I took a few rides, excited to be traveling in the swinging metal car hundreds of feet above the outlying neighborhoods of the city, along with groups of blasé working-class Colombians who were just using it to get home. They spent the journey on their phones in a style that was new to me: using WhatsApp, they'd record short blurbs, then send them. Moments later, an answer would come in another voice memo. They'd respond, and so on and so on. I later learned that this was cheaper than making live calls and compensated for sometimes spotty reception. It was a sort-of-live conversation, and it seemed to work perfectly well.

**Newsletters**, professional or informal, are used by professionals in certain types of businesses—consultants, coaches, educators, personal trainers, authors, journalists, even lawyers and doctors—to communicate with their clients and broader network. In the service sector, this falls under the category of "content marketing." You are trying to remind your customers why they like you and to further establish yourself a source of useful information.[2]

If your business has some type of newsletter or email blast function, you might consider how to improve it. Take a look at the ones you receive and identify the ones that you actually like: What do you like about them? Is it the voice, the content, the design? How do you feel about the frequency? Take a look at the ones you ignore or delete: What's wrong with their approach? What advice would you give them about how to connect with you better?

## The Art of the Ping

Guess what: you can send messages with no expectation of a reply. This category could also be titled, "Hi, I'm alive, no response required." This is my *favorite* category, and it may soon become yours because it's easy, it's human, and it works.

Here are a few examples:

- "Hey, I was thinking about you. I hope you are well."
- "I wanted to share some news. Check out this short blurb about my new job! Hope all is good."
- "I was reading this article and thought of you."

---

2. This is a bit different from retail stores that barrage you with emails about sales and product offers. There, the value is simply making you aware of something you might want to buy.

These messages accomplish something. They remind people you exist. They remind them of their positive feelings about you. They may trigger other associations—a project, an opportunity, a connection.

Many people will respond to these messages, but they understand they don't have to, and that makes a big difference. In our world, it's a relief to know *we don't have one more task to do.* Most of us live in a world of inboxes that keep growing, endless chores, piles of work that get no smaller, and people we need to get back to. You are making life easy for your contacts—maintaining connection while letting them off the hook for doing something. When someone conveys, "I was thinking of you but no need to reply," it is a gem.

Again, *you can send a message without requesting that the other person do anything.*

This is "the art of the ping." (A ping is a tech-world term for just nonobnoxiously poking at people. "Hi, it's me." "Hi, I'm alive." "Hi, I like you.")

## Examples:

### Professional Update
Dear Stephanie,

Happy New Year! I hope you have been well considering all we've been through the past few years. I recently moved to Citigroup, and so far, it's great! I hope you and the girls are doing well. Would love to catch up at some point.

–Monique

### Old Friend
Dear Kev,

I was passing my gym (formerly "our" gym) and thought of you. I miss having a workout buddy, but I trust things are going well for you in Arizona. I still plan to get out there in the not too distant future, and if so, I will take you up on your offer of margaritas. In the meantime, stay well.

—George ("The Juice")

### Topics of Interest
Dear Rajindra,

I was reading the *Wall Street Journal* and came across this article about celebrity-related NFTs. You were the first person I ever heard using the phrase "NFT," so naturally I thought of you. I hope all is well.

—Carole

### Personal Aspect of Business Development
Dear Hector,

My twins just turned seven. Okay, twist my arm, here is a photo. I assume we will see each other again when the next deal is up for negotiation, but in the meantime just wanted to say hey. By the way, I'm still on team keto. Thanks for the push.

—Oswaldo

### Passing on Useful Information
Dear Ms. Takashima,

Best wishes for the holiday season. We have really enjoyed working with your team over the past years. We have recently put out a new white paper on EMEA compliance issues. Here is the link in case you might find it of interest. The basic takeaway is: be alert, not worried.

I hope your family is well.

—Jackie Park

**Reminder of Former Connection**

Dear Friends,

I'm not sure if you heard it yet, but Saundra just started her MBA. I'm attaching her latest update. She is super excited, as am I. Thanks again for your participation in our fan group all these years. Hope all is well.

—Melanie

## How to Make It Happen and Keep It Going: Systems for Maintaining Contacts and Staying in Contact

To keep the whole effort going, you have to solve for two things:

1. how you are going to reach out; and
2. how you will keep track of everything.

You need a system, which is another way of saying you need a set of habits.

Habits reduce cognitive load and reduce fatigue. You don't have to decide everything on a discretionary basis.

### Start with Who You Are... Mostly

For outreach, plan your efforts based on who you are . . . plus a bit of stretch.

This means that if you're a confirmed introvert, feel free to focus on activities that are more comfortable for introverts—plus the occasional activity requiring more extroversion. Pick one-on-one meetings, not cocktail parties. Set things up by email rather than picking up the phone. Have conversations through email or text rather than live. Go to the occasional event, but agree to meet a friend there and decide ahead of time how long you will stay.

On the other hand, if you're an action-seeking extrovert, pick up the phone. Invite people for group drinks. Make a list of people you want to meet at the conference. (If you're an introvert going to the same conference, have a shorter list and send short emails ahead of time letting them know you'll be looking out for them.)

*You can be successful at growing your network without needing to be someone else.* Most people do almost no networking and are terrible at building relationships. Making any intentional effort is better than making no effort, and being thoughtful already puts you ahead of the game.

## Decide on Some Habits

A habit is something you do regularly, without asking whether you should. Another word we use is *structure*—a method of device you use.

Here are some examples of structures:

- Spend ten minutes each day reviewing LinkedIn—checking what jobs people are in, reading and commenting on postings, or adding new connections
- Set up one breakfast a week
- Follow a rule about saying "yes" to school volunteering
- Have brunch once a month at your house with a revolving list of attendees
- Check in with ten to fifteen friends from college and business school once every three months
- Try to set up at least one client dinner per transaction, matter, or fiscal quarter
- Spend time in airports and on planes writing catch-up emails
- Make a list of twelve people you want to know better over the course of the year and set up a lunch once a month
- Keep a copy of your twins' latest adorable photos on your laptop and phone and frequently send them as attachments or texts (Hey, that's me!)

## Make a Simple Tracking System

A good tracking system captures two things:

1.  the names and contact information for people in your invisible net-
    work, and
2.  how much you contact them.

My view on data systems is that if you enjoy them, you probably already
have one. And if you don't enjoy them, it will be difficult for you to maintain
new ones, unless they are extremely simple. Hence, I recommend the most
basic one that will get the job done, and the job is defined as just having
some sense of who your contacts are and of your efforts to keep in touch
with them.

Here are some options:

**Bingo card collection.** Keep track of your Relationship Portfolio Bingo
Cards each month. It's an easy way to track where you've made efforts. If you
make hard copies, you can easily fit them into a file folder or box, and if you
use electronic versions, you can put them in a folder. There is satisfaction in
seeing them grow.

**LinkedIn.** The easiest way to keep up with professional contacts is
LinkedIn. As long as a person keeps their profile reasonably up to date,
you know what they are doing and you normally have their current email
address. You can also message them directly.

LinkedIn also makes it easy to share articles and comment (positively)
on people's posts. Since you have to request connections, and people either
accept or don't, it's a low-stress way to extend yourself. It has a different vibe
from other social media platforms. It's more work-oriented, and people tend
to stay uncontroversial. It's easy to know how to behave.

**Outlook/Gmail/other email programs.** You can use your email program
as a way to track your contacts. The key is to have a regular method of turning email addresses into names in your contacts file. You could open up

a contact each time you receive or send an important email, make a habit of consolidating once a week or once a month, or charge an assistant with doing this for you. This doesn't solve the problem of keeping track of how often you're reaching out, but at least you have valid contact information.

**CRM/contact management systems.** Salesforce, SharpSpring, Raiser's Edge, and similar programs are designed to consolidate your contacts and tie them to actions you take to reach out. These are complex tools with numerous bells and whistles. You may be using them already, either because your work requires it or you have a high level of skill and interest in maintaining systems like these. My belief is that if you aren't using them already, there's a reason, and there are probably simpler tools available to you.

**Holiday card list.** You can use the annual holiday greeting card as a tool to keep your contacts together. You can do a modern, automated system where you drop in a list of contacts and a central server sends out your cards, or you can go super old school, like me, and send out handwritten versions. The benefit of this is that there's a forcing function: you need to get these out by a certain date, other people do the same, and it requires you to catch yourself up on your existing contacts.

**Fundraising list.** If you join a nonprofit board, one of the first things you'll be asked to is to come up with your "list." This is a list of your contacts that the organization will send fundraising pleas to. Every year you'll be asked to check and update your list.

This is sort of a pain, but it can work for you. Like the holiday card, it has a forcing function that requires you to get your act together.[3]

---

3. If you are supposed to raise funds with your "list," my advice is to not overthink it and send a fundraising request to everyone you know. Fundraising has mostly moved online, so it is no more costly to send out five hundred requests than fifty, and you never know who will say yes. Also, always make sure to include vendors you've hired on your appeal list—lawyers, PR agencies, accountants, contractors, and people like me. Professionals who receive money from you usually have the good sense to keep the flow going.

**Notebooks, Filofax, etc.** If you're using handwritten tools to organize your contacts, power to you. There's a lot to be said for tactile connections to the people in your invisible network, so that everything isn't contained in electronic files nested in electronic files nested in electronic files. The trick is to make sure you have some central place to store all this. You might have a folder, a desk drawer, or a pile of stuff somewhere. So long as you know where it is and you can work with it, it's a good technique.

I'll close this section with a word of caution: Do figure out a way to capture the names and contact information for the people in your life. Don't think you will "catch up" at some future date.

I am a cautionary tale! I've been doing intimate, important work with amazing clients for twenty years. I consider myself an organized person, but before writing this book, I would have given myself a C-minus for the quality of my contact information. I had just never created a regular system for tracking people (other than searching through old emails). It was only because nowadays you need to have a firm marketing plan to get any kind of nonfiction book deal that I finally created a workable system. This is a case of do what I say, not what I did.

## The Value of Acknowledging Important Events (and the Ones You Can Skip)

I want to close out this section with a discussion of the special value of acknowledging important events. This is true of all relationships, but I'm putting it in this chapter because this is one situation where you want to be more deliberate about connecting with your weak ties, rather than just reaching out when you feel like it. I'll then list the ones I think you can skip.

The following are some situations that most people find especially meaningful. Life calls on you to respond and acknowledge certain things, including for people who you've fallen out of touch with.

## Birthdays

I am not a big birthday person. But I have come to understand that birthdays are important to a lot of people. Saying "happy birthday" makes a difference and is easy. So do it. If you want to take it to the next level, make a phone call or send an actual card.

## Accomplishments

Congratulate people who have big accomplishments, whether private or public. If it's something they have strived for or they have achieved a level of public acclaim, your acknowledgment will always be welcome. Some accomplishments have a once-in-a-lifetime quality. You might think that people tire of hearing praise, but they don't. You might think that if they are famous, or written about in the press, they don't need another voice chiming in. This is not true.

## Illnesses

When someone is seriously ill, reach out and tell them you're thinking of them and wish them well. If you're planning on sending a text or Facebook message, you can do better. Pick up the phone, write a card or letter, send a package, visit them in person, or if they are in seclusion, drop something off. Don't say, "Let me know if I can do anything." That's just giving them a job. Do something.

Do people just want their privacy in these situations? Yes and no. I don't think anyone wants an identity as "the sick person," but if they are in fact sick or dealing with a life-threatening illness, they are vulnerable, scared, and most likely down in the dumps.

If someone I know has cancer, I write a card or letter. I've done this for a colleague, for a client, and for a neighbor down the road whose family hangs up right-wing flags. They all contacted me afterwards. It was noticed. At least one of them kept the card for years afterwards. It's a simple thing, but where it's not done much in this age, it makes a difference.

## Deaths

When your colleague or friend experiences the death of someone, acknowledge it. If they post a lengthy message on Facebook about their parent or grandparent or friend, write a short note of appreciation for what they said. Give them a call. Write a card or letter.

If someone has a wake or is sitting shiva, and you are invited or told about it, go. You don't have to stay for a long time; you just need to make the effort. Sometimes life is just being with people.

## Births

Many cultures have elaborate rituals and ceremonies around births and important dates in baby and child development. For most people they are a huge celebration without compare.

When someone in your life has a baby, go and visit the baby. Sooner is better than later. You contact the person and say you would like to come visit. Don't wait for an invitation. Don't wait until it's convenient for you. A newborn is *Hamilton*, and your job is try to get a ticket. You might not be successful—new parents have to manage the limited time they have, it's risky to expose newborns to germs until they are fifty-nine days old, and there are a lot of friends and relatives in their lives. But give the new parents that option.

I was late to learn this. It wasn't until I had my own sons that I realized how meaningful this was. Before, I might have thought, *What do they need me for?* But I found myself paying careful attention to who reached out and wanted to visit, who showed up, how they behaved (stay a bit, but not too long), and in particular who did not come, or who scheduled and canceled several times. There are four men in my life who I basically cut from my friends list because they could not get it together to see my babies when they were young. There was a fifth, but we had a discussion and resolved it a couple of years later.

Is this petty? Maybe, maybe not. When I became a dad, my values shifted.

A final word on this: if you're a man married to a woman, don't leave it for your wife to suggest or arrange all of this, especially if it's your own colleague who has given birth. And if you're a single guy, don't wait until you are one day married to engage in this kind of social connection.

Man up, and go see that baby.

## The Things You Don't Need to Do or Attend

Here are some things that, in my book, you don't have to do:

**Weddings.** Weddings can be nice, but they are also a huge time and money sink. Unless you are a member of the wedding party or a key person in the life of the couple (boss, best friend, beloved next-door neighbor), you don't have to attend. Send a gift.

**Fundraising events.** It's nice to attend fundraising events for your friends' causes, and you get credit for showing up. However, you can also skip the event and just make a donation.

**Large group dinners in restaurants.** When you're in your twenties and thirties, it's common to be invited to group restaurant events of eight to twenty-plus people. These get tiresome very quickly—conversation is hard, and the "let's divide the check evenly" business can lead to bad feelings. You can skip these.

**Concerts and shows.** You're allowed to skip loud concerts, shows that you're not interested in, or venues that are physically uncomfortable (bad bathroom, overly crowded, etc.).

**Multilevel marketing events.** You may on occasion be invited to a multilevel marketing (MLM) event. These are businesses that distribute goods through social networks—examples are Tupperware, Mary Kay, Herbalife, and Amway. There are new ones all the time. You can find other ways to support your friends' ambitions besides participating these events.

**Each day of a professional event or conference.** Conferences can be great to attend, but you don't need to go each day. Try attending for just one day, or even half a day.

## TWENTY-MINUTES-A-DAY EXERCISES

- **Exercise 1:** Go to a card store and buy a few birthday cards, along with a "thinking of you" card and a sympathy card—and anything else that strikes your fancy. Keep them at your desk for future use.
- **Exercise 2:** Send out two ping emails, modeled after the scripts in this chapter.
- **Exercise 3:** Recall the last interesting article you've read. It doesn't have to be heavy. It could be a celebrity listicle if you liked it. Forward the article to someone in your network, with a "Thinking of you, thought you might enjoy this" message.

# PART 3
# Leveraging Relationships

# CHAPTER 10

# Understanding Your Needs and Knowing What to Ask For

You'll recall that my sons were born through a process of in vitro fertilization and surrogacy.

As birth approached, because Baby A was not in the right position—he was "frank," or seated rather than head down—the OB-GYN scheduled a C-section on the Monday that would have been their thirty-sixth week in the womb.

I was at my gym one afternoon when Caitlin, our surrogate, called from her car. Her contractions had increased. She called the doctor and he recommended that she come to the hospital. "They want to know when you can get here," she said.

"Oh, you mean in the next few days?"

"I think they mean right now. They want to do the C-section tomorrow morning."

Yikes. "Okay, then!"

A few minutes later, I'd purchased passage for a flight later that night from New York to Minneapolis, and then on to Sioux Falls, South Dakota.

I totally wasn't ready for this! And I don't just mean psychologically; I mean logistically as well. The crib wasn't assembled. My closet was in the middle of being outfitted with shelves. I had one car seat but not two. I had no supplies of any kind. I'd interviewed a baby nurse I liked but hadn't scheduled anything. I knew the babies were coming, but I'd figured I had a few more days to work things out. My home was not equipped for newborn twins, and I had to get on a plane in three hours.

Samuel Johnson famously said, "When a man knows he is to be hanged in a fortnight, it concentrates his mind wonderfully." Along those lines, knowing that twin newborns were going to enter my life in a matter of hours made me much better at asking for help.

I asked my operations director, Zach, to get my keys and oversee everything that needed to be done. I asked my cleaning lady to ask her husband to assemble the crib. I asked my mother to fly from California to South Dakota to visit me. I asked my sister if she would help bring the babies back from South Dakota. I took a month off from work meetings and asked my colleagues to bear with me. I asked most of my clients to take a breather. The time crunch made visible how other people could help me. It also removed any mental barriers I had to asking for help.

The next morning my beautiful twin sons were born at thirty-five and a half weeks and in perfect health. I've done a lot more asking since then.

People think that asking is hard because they don't want to seem grabby or selfish or just too much. I think we have the opposite problem: we don't ask for enough, mainly because we haven't really thought out what our needs are or the many ways other people could help us be more successful.

To know what to ask for, you must know your needs. And then you have to jab yourself and ask what else you need. Leveraging your relationships requires that you know yourself better.

In this chapter we'll look at this *what* you might want to ask for, and in the next, we'll demystify *how* you actually make the ask.

## Obvious and Nonobvious Needs

You have some needs that are obvious to you. You know what is missing and you are aware that it exists out there in the world somewhere. The preface here is "I need . . ." Examples of obvious needs are:

- A better job
- A new manager for my marketing department
- A good IP lawyer
- A babysitter for Friday night

You're looking for a solution. You can step back one step and think about the information that might help you find this solution. Let's call these informational or advisory needs. This might include thoughts on where to look for a better job, advice on the best way to recruit a new manager, referrals for lawyers, or information on babysitting resources.

You can take an additional step back and *broaden* how you are looking at each need. There might be multiple ways to address a need—do you need leads for a new marketing manager, or do you need a better interview process? Or perhaps the real issue may be different from the presenting issue—are you looking for a new job, or are you frustrated with your current job? These are not the same thing.

The more broadly you look, the more you will see different ways people could help you. This then affects what you might ask for.

| Specific Need | Broader Frame for Ways Others Can Help |
|---|---|
| Get a new job | • Ideas for networking groups<br>• Feedback on résumé<br>• Discussion with boss about future path at current company |
| Hire marketing manager | • Referrals for recruiters<br>• Get colleague to head search process<br>• Team meeting for ways we can work around open position |
| Lawyer recommendation | • Referral for lawyer<br>• Discussions with other start-up people about legal and business issues and things to look out for<br>• Yoga classes or other resources for work/life balance (to avoid getting overstressed by unresolved work issues) |
| Find babysitter | • Referral for babysitter<br>• Advice from other working parents about how to manage childcare<br>• Advice from other working parents about dealing with guilt |

One function of a coach, mentor, therapist, or friend is to help you broaden your thinking. You might go to them expecting to get an answer to a specific ask, but the real value may be in how they help you to expand your thinking in terms of what might actually help you.

## Exercise: Brainstorming How Others Could Help You

Pick two important goals. For the purposes of this exercise, try to make them dissimilar: one might be work-related, and one might be personal. Or one might seem highly feasible, and the other might seem more fantastical. Then answer the questions below.

## Goal 1 (description):

**Questions:**

1.  What's the best-case scenario for help other people could give you?
2.  What's the average scenario?
3.  What are the different ways other people might weigh in or help?
4.  What are one or two obvious requests you're willing to make of people?

## Goal 2 (description):

**Questions:**

1.  What's the best-case scenario for help other people could give you?
2.  What's the average scenario?
3.  What are the different ways other people might weigh in or help?
4.  What are one or two obvious requests you're willing to make of people?

## *Examples*

| **Goal 1:** Write bestseller | **Description:** Write and market a bestselling business book that changes lives, makes me a star, and creates a long-term income stream |
| --- | --- |
| 1. What's the best-case scenario for help other people could give you? | I write it. I do events to market it (fun!). Other people fill in all the pieces that allow me to do this: email list, newsletter production, web stuff, finding conferences, getting on podcasts, and everything required to do a ton of corporate events that does not strictly require my own labor. Basically, I would I just write the book and promote it and meet lots of cool new people while continuing my normal income-generating work activities. |
| 2. What's the average scenario? | People take some things off my plate, I still lead the army and do some grunt work, but I can rely on people for specific things. People also help me break things down (e.g., how to build an email list, creating strategy for reaching out to client organizations to do group talks, etc.). |

| 3. What are the different ways other people might weigh in or help? | Cathy: be overall task manager<br>New contractor: find someone who specializes in content repurposing (breaking down book and podcast ideas into smaller forms suitable for different media)<br>Gretchen: give advice on how to use superfans to push out the word<br>Marci: strategy on conferences<br>Barbara and Sharon: more childcare hours<br>M and H: take the lead on work projects to free up my time |
| --- | --- |
| 4. Obvious asks | Cathy: handle email list management process, or identify someone I can outsource this to<br>Barbara and Sharon: more childcare hours |

| **Goal 2:** Super kids | **Description:** Raise my children to be educated, bilingual, and lovers of reading and music, while being mentally healthy and enjoying their childhood |
| --- | --- |
| 1. What's the best-case scenario for help other people could give you? | Give me perfect advice, watch them so I don't have to worry, give me wisdom on activities that are going to be most interesting and fulfilling for my kids |
| 2. What's the average scenario? | I meet like-minded parents and share tips with them. I can get referrals on lessons and outsource some of the learning. I can bond with parents about hard parts rather than suffering alone. |
| 3. What are the different ways other people might weigh in or help? | • Stacey, Courtney, and other moms: advice<br>• Continue video Spanish lessons with Alberto 2–3 times a week<br>• Referrals for art or dance programs<br>• Find "fun" babysitter who can help them with homework and play games<br>• Crowdsource summer camp ideas, by target age |

| 4. Obvious asks | • Make list of three to five moms/parents I like talking to and call them<br>• Ask Alberto to lay out expected trajectory of their language learning<br>• Ask 5–10 parents with older kids what summer activities their kids did when younger |
| --- | --- |

## TWENTY-MINUTES-A-DAY EXERCISES

- **Exercise 1:** Think back and try to write down what you've asked people for over the past month. Consider work colleagues, clients, family, friends, and all kinds of service providers (such as restaurant servers, store clerks, auto repair technicians, customer assistance lines, etc.). Do you ask for too much, too little, or the right amount? Do you ask once or persist? Are there people you find easier to ask for things than others? What accounts for the difference?

- **Exercise 2:** The next time you plan to meet a friend or colleague, come up with a different ask in terms of location. If you meet for coffee, ask to go for a walk instead. If you meet for drinks, ask to meet for breakfast. If you normally Zoom, ask to talk by phone or meet in person.

- **Exercise 3:** One way you can think of people in your life is as "As" and "Bs." As give you energy, and Bs take away energy. My recommendations are to (1) spend as much time as possible with As, and (2) tell Bs exactly what you need from them, rather than waiting for them to guess. For this activity, make a list of five As in your life. Reach out to one of them and ask to have a chat or spend some time together. You can hear more about this idea by listening to my podcast episode on As and Bs. You can listen directly at this URL: careerstewardship.com/bonus-episode. You can also find it on any podcast app—look for *Career Stewardship with Michael Melcher*. It's a bonus episode sandwiched between episodes 17 and 18.

# CHAPTER 11
## Expanding Your Ask

Meghan Daum is a writer who achieved literary distinction at a young age. She published a brilliant and hilarious set of essays, *My Misspent Youth,* and soon thereafter a comic novel. She's the kind of writer who has appeared in the *New Yorker* and teaches at the kinds of writing programs people are eager to get into. But in the past few years, she's made a big shift—or, more precisely, a big shift has been pushed on her, and she has adapted.

First, the historical model of journalism collapsed, as online news aggregators like Google and Facebook crushed the traditional news organs that actually created content. Second, the political landscape shifted. She had a hard time getting published. Her writing was suddenly considered too provocative. On a variety of topics, it challenged the reasoning of the newly ascendant gatekeepers at media outlets like the *New York Times* and National Public Radio. Meghan didn't think that her own views had changed at all. She was still a freethinking, left-of-center feminist. But others disputed that.

She started a podcast, *The Unspeakable,* named after one of her books. It was dedicated to talking about, with nuance, things that didn't make it into most public conversations. She didn't want to come up with a "take" about a current issue, but instead wanted to have deep conversations where you could not predict at the outset what the conclusions would be. This was also a new business. It costs money to run a podcast, but you can also make money if you can amass a set of paying subscribers on Patreon, Substack, or similar platforms. You can make a living without being approved by gate-keepers. In theory. The execution of making-a-good-living was hard and there was no script.

I'm a huge fan of Meghan Daum and her work. I wondered if she would consider being on my own podcast, *Career Stewardship with Michael Melcher,* and do a real-life, unscripted coaching conversation, where I would be the coach and she would be the client. Despite my repeated refrain that you should ask people for things, and in particular ask things of your weak ties, it took me maybe two months between having this idea and sending her a request by email. She said yes. Her coachable issue would be "money" and, specifically, how to make more of it.

I stepped out of my role of fan and into my role of professional coach. I asked her a series of open-ended questions about what she'd learned about doing business, how long she assumed it would take to be successful, and what she needed to do to get there. We ran into some assumptions about asking.

Meghan had a revulsion for asking others for anything.

"I've always been this way," she explained. Her family, as well. "Hallow-een was fraught—the idea of going around asking for free candy horrified my parents. And selling Girl Scout Cookies—that was just impossible. My par-ents raised us to depend on ourselves, and I've always depended on myself."

I asked her how she thought other people might feel if she made requests. She didn't know. We went on to talk about her Patreon community—these were people who listened to the (free) podcast but also voluntarily paid a monthly amount to support her and get other benefits.[1] She was going to have a Zoom hangout where these like-minded people could meet her and

---

1. She has since moved to Substack, which has the same type of patron programs.

each other and talk about issues raised by the podcast. I probed about what role this community might play in her own success: Specifically, was she assuming that success was all up to her? Or could other people help her?

This was a new line of thinking for her. She had felt responsible for doing everything. It was a new idea that others might help her, if she was willing to ask them.

Some of her audience listened to our episode. After this conversation, one of the Patreon patrons commented in a chat platform, "Meghan, at the last hangout we asked you how we could help. You still haven't answered us."

Meghan Daum had a need. She had a network of people who appreciated her work and who wanted to help. But for real success to come, she needed to make the ask—for them to reach out to their friends, to promote her show, even to move to higher levels of sponsorship. That required both action and soul-searching. It required her to do some things that would make her uncomfortable, maybe extremely uncomfortable.

In this chapter, we cover ways to make asks in emails, by phone, and in meetings. We also analyze the elements of negotiations, since you may need to ask for something besides what is being offered. We'll examine why we should focus on the other party's underlying interests and not just their stated position. We will also do some exercises that train you to respond to yes/no questions.

## Rules for Asking

Here are three rules for asking:

1. You're allowed to ask for things.
2. You get things by asking for them.
3. You can negotiate.

People are allowed to respond the way they want. They have free agency, just as you do. You can't control them and don't have to. Let's go through each of these.

## You're Allowed to Ask

Desiree Portillo-Rabinov grew up in a working-class Chicano community in Los Angeles. In junior high, she was offered a slot in a voluntary busing program that would take her to a school in an affluent, largely White part of the San Fernando Valley. She took the chance with her brother. She learned a lot. One lesson was that her fellow classmates and their parents *asked* for things.

"They were very assertive and didn't take no for an answer. There was always another solution." This approach was quite different from how she'd been raised. Desiree picked up on this direct communication style, and the knowledge changed her life.

Many people feel inhibited when it comes to asking for things. They feel they don't have permission, or it would seem aggressive, or they are afraid of rejection. But really, when you ask for something, all the other person can say is no, or ask you to clarify, or ask you to convince them otherwise.

You're allowed to ask.

## You Get Things by Asking for Them

It would be nice if other people would provide what we want without our asking for it.

Just FYI, the world doesn't work this way. Let's be specific.

**Other people are not spending all their time thinking of you.** People are not thinking about you; they are mostly thinking about themselves. Even if you have an intense conversation with them, when it's done, their attention will shift to other things.

**The other person may be inclined to say yes, but probably won't until you ask.** Others are taking their cues from you. If you haven't asked, they may conclude something is not important to you. If you haven't asked yet, they may conclude you don't need it yet. Your ask is their "activation moment."

**"You get the sale by asking for the sale."** There is a saying in sales that you get the sale by asking for the sale. The ask is what prompts people to make a yes or no decision, or negotiate for something else.

**Sometimes you're competing against the other people who _do_ ask.** In general, I believe there is enough to go around and that someone's win is not your loss. But sometimes it is useful to think of the competition. The world includes people who are assertive, who look out for their interests, and who don't let discomfort stop them. Squeaky wheels do sometimes get the grease, so if you stay stoic and silent, you can lose out.

## You Can Negotiate

Young Desiree learned that "there was always another option." If someone makes a request or offer, you can say yes, no, or make a counteroffer.

| Offer | Counteroffer (Other Option) |
|---|---|
| • "Let's see this Iranian film that won an Oscar." | • "I don't like subtitles, but a movie sounds fun. How about we see Jennifer Garner's new movie?" |
| • "We'd like your child to get tested by our school specialist. We are concerned about his behavior." | • "I'm going to take him to a clinician that a friend referred me to. Then I'll get back to you." |
| • "We're giving you a raise of 3 percent." | • "Thank you. I think that a raise in the neighborhood of 5 to 8 percent reflects the value I've been adding. How does that sound?" |
| • "Let's set up a call. Does Zoom work for you?" | • "I'm going to be near your office tomorrow—how about we take a fifteen-minute walk around your block? I can pick up coffee for you beforehand." |

| | |
|---|---|
| • "I'd love you to come to my destination wedding in Dubai. It will be a week of amazing fun with all our friends from business school." | • "How wonderful! We won't be attending, but I'd love to contribute to your honeymoon fund. Is there a link?" |
| • "The class is full, and we don't keep waiting lists." | • "I'll wait outside, and in case someone doesn't show up, the teacher can decide whether to let me in." |

Any back-and-forth between two people is a negotiation. When two people negotiate, they are working through what will be a satisfactory outcome for both. In a negotiation, what is important is the end point, not the starting point. (In chapter seventeen, we'll go more deeply into the topic of reacting to requests and setting boundaries.)

Negotiation isn't bad. It's good. Negotiation isn't being pushy. It's showing respect. You can view it as a team effort to find the solution that will satisfy both of you.

In my twenties, I spent a year in India with the State Department. One weekend I traveled to Jaipur with a State Department colleague named Debbi. Jaipur is a beautiful, historic city in Rajasthan. I had heard that Rajasthan is where I would be able to buy those fantastic embroidered slippers, the kind that twirl up at the toe.

We wandered around the colorful market, and I found some footwear that struck my fancy. I asked the salesman how much they cost, and he quoted an amount of rupees that was equivalent to a few bucks. I knew that I was negotiation was expected, but I accepted the price. They were cheap for me, and I didn't want to be a jerk.

Debbi was appalled at my lack of market savvy. I explained that I felt bad fussing over an amount I could easily afford. I didn't want to take advantage of a humble vendor of twirly slippers.

"He does this all day," Debbi said. "He's done this for years. He doesn't need your pity. Do you think you know more about his profit margins than he does? You couldn't take advantage of him if you tried."

That made sense, but wouldn't he be happy to earn more?

"If you'd had a protracted negotiation, he could have gone home and said, 'Yeah, this American came in and thought he knew what was doing, but I showed him what was up.' But he can't have that satisfaction now. He's more likely to think that he blew it. If you were such an easy mark, he regrets not starting with a higher price.

"The other thing you're missing is that in traditional societies, bargaining is a social interaction. You're used to going to a store where you just see a price and pay it or not. There's no interaction. But here, bargaining is a way to connect with people and get to know them. If you don't bargain, you miss all that. It's a lot more fun and meaningful than just walking into a store and buying something off the shelf."

Negotiation isn't haggling. Negotiation allows you to be more precise about needs and value. The first thing someone offers you is often their first guess about what they can do for you or their first thought about how the two of you will interact in your relationship. If you give them more information, they might offer something else, not because you are *getting* more from them, but because they have a better idea how to meet your needs.

You can ask for a higher salary or raise than you are offered. You can ask for different, more, or fewer hours. You can ask for an earlier appointment. You can ask to see a new set of designs. You can ask for a different role on the fundraising committee. You can ask your coach, therapist, or personal trainer to go in a different direction.

And in each of these scenarios, the other person can respond—and come back to you with a yes, a no, or a counteroffer. You might not get what you want. They might not get what they want. The negotiation could end with no agreement. That doesn't mean you are permanently ostracized from the rest of humanity. It just means you didn't quite get what you wanted. Life doesn't need to be a "take it or leave it" experience. Ask for things, see what happens, and then stay in the dialogue.

## The Art: Different Ways of Asking for Things

Asking is an art. What works best varies by the situation.

One simple framework is to categorize requests from direct to indirect and from specific to general.

1(a)    When you ask directly, you are asking a person to do something.

- "Can you introduce me to a bankruptcy partner at Williams & Kelly?"

1(b)    When you ask indirectly, you are expressing your needs to someone who may be able to help, but you aren't asking directly.

- "One of my objectives is to speak with a bankruptcy partner at Williams & Kelly."

2(a)    When you ask specifically, you are naming what you need. You're signaling to the person that you desire a particular outcome that they might be able to address.

- "Specifically, I'd like to speak with bankruptcy partners at major law firms, especially those who lateraled from other firms."

2(b)    When you ask generally, you put forth a broad set of ways you could be helped. You are signaling to the person that they can address any of the needs in that broad set or sometimes go in a different direction.

- "I'm interested in building relationships with lawyers who work in bankruptcy and understand how the business landscape is changing in this area. I'm also really curious about your own path and what you've learned about being successful and happy in a large law firm environment. Any of those would be really useful for me, or we could go in another direction."

Here is a matrix for understanding what is going on:

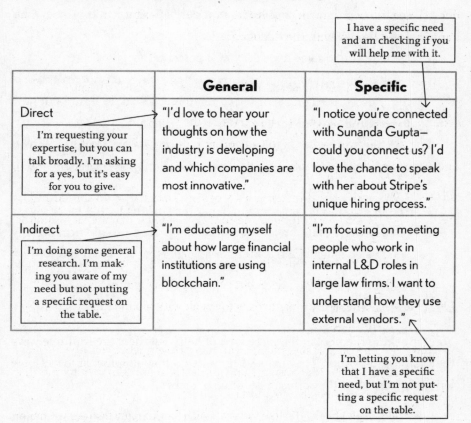

|  | **General** | **Specific** |
|---|---|---|
| Direct<br><br>I'm requesting your expertise, but you can talk broadly. I'm asking for a yes, but it's easy for you to give. | "I'd love to hear your thoughts on how the industry is developing and which companies are most innovative." | "I notice you're connected with Sunanda Gupta—could you connect us? I'd love the chance to speak with her about Stripe's unique hiring process." |
| Indirect<br><br>I'm doing some general research. I'm making you aware of my need but not putting a specific request on the table. | "I'm educating myself about how large financial institutions are using blockchain." | "I'm focusing on meeting people who work in internal L&D roles in large law firms. I want to understand how they use external vendors." |

*I have a specific need and am checking if you will help me with it.*

*I'm letting you know that I have a specific need, but I'm not putting a specific request on the table.*

## Ways to Ask with Scripts

Let's go over some specific scripts.

### Direct, Specific Request

You have a specific request, and you are clearly letting the other person know you would like their response.

- "Would you be willing to make an introduction to Kayla?"
- "Could you forward my bio and résumé to your contact at Netflix?"

- "I'd like to have an initial conversation with the people who run coaching programs and leadership development at Coca-Cola. Can you make an introduction for me?"
- "I'd like you to raise my salary by 8 percent."
- "I'd like you to read my article, then tell me where it's not really working. I don't need praise or encouragement. I want to figure out how to fix it and make it really good."
- "I'd like you to be a co-host at my political event. This means you would invite five people and make a donation of at least $500. It will be fun! How about it?"
- "I'd like you to be my mentor. What that means is that twice a year or so we'd meet for breakfast and catch up. And I might occasionally send you a short email asking for advice. How does that sound?

## Direct, General Request

You are asking the person for some type of help, but there are multiple ways they could satisfy that. They can use their discretion about what to say, how long to speak, what they offer to do, and so forth.

- "I'd love to hear your thoughts on how the industry is developing and which companies are most innovative."
- "I'd love to pick your brain about the start-up scene in Chicago."
- "I want to make a transition from engineering to the business side. You've done that, and I'd like to learn more about your experience."
- "I'd like to learn more about how consultants get good at business development. I'd appreciate hearing what you've tried over the years."
- "I'd like to describe my relationship with Michael and just get your reaction."

- "My niece just graduated from SMU and is going to start in Accenture. I think she could use some resources on how to start off right. Any ideas you have would be welcome."
- "You just did a huge renovation. I'm just starting mine. What did you learn?"

## Indirect, Specific Request

This is a special category: you'd really like the person to do something, but you don't want to put them on the spot. This is a face-saving approach—they might solve your problem, but if they don't, neither of you need to feel awkward.

- "At this point in my biz dev strategy, I'm focusing on meeting people in start-ups that outsourced their HR functions. I want to understand how they decide on vendors."
- "I'm setting up meetings with the professional development departments of major law firms. These are getting to know each other conversations with the people who handle training, coaching, diversity, and professional development."
- "We'd like to add someone with a technology background to our board. Basically, someone with a set of qualifications similar to yours. I'm interested in learning how this type of individual would think about nonprofit board service."
- "Based on how you've described your colleagues, I think I have a lot in common with the coaches at your firm. You represent the type of firm I imagined when I started this transition."
- "One thing I'm focusing on now is identifying connections who work in product development in FAANG companies. Ideally, I'd like to start by speaking with people at Apple."

## *Indirect, General Request*

This is the most open request—you're identifying various ways others might help you, without putting the other person on the spot. Yet you're not overly vague—you are still providing clear guidance for how they can be successful in the conversation.

- "I'm educating myself about how large financial institutions are using blockchain."
- "I'm curious how coaching firms like yours would regard someone of my background."
- "I've been talking to great minds about how they've managed their own career transitions and what advice they would give to someone currently in this process."
- "I'm exploring doing my own investing or partnering with someone else to build a firm."
- "I'm upskilling myself in terms of basic management. I love hearing about resources, techniques, and models people have found useful, particularly people like me who came from a very technical field and then found themselves managing people."

## The Costs of What You're Asking For

Consider what the cost of meeting your request is to the other person. This is not always obvious.

Something that could benefit you greatly might cost the other person nothing (e.g., a recommendation for an inexpensive, high-quality pre-K program, or a copy of a slide deck from an interesting presentation). Other times, meeting your request may cost the other person something, but they are willing to do it or they get a benefit from doing it (e.g., making an introduction to a significant contact). Yet other times, the cost of what you are asking might be too high for them (e.g., making a personal recommendation to the hiring committee or bringing their family to dinner to meet yours).

## Improving Your Skill at Being Silent

Once you make a specific ask, *stop talking*. Give the other person time to process what you are saying and respond. You can ruin a good ask by nervously filling in the silence. Compare:

- "I'm requesting a 10 percent raise starting January 1. I just feel really strongly about this. I know you have a lot on your mind. Is that date okay? Probably you think the timing of this is bad. But this is important and I'm not going to be unappreciated anymore and gaslit about my value. But I'm not trying to put pressure on you."
- "I'm requesting a 10 percent raise starting January 1."

Silence feels longer when you are doing the asking than it does for the person receiving the request. They are actually thinking—let them have their process. When they start to respond, don't interrupt.

## Don't Muddle Your Request to Seem Nice

You can muddle your messages by adding unnecessary or confusing words to a request. Compare:

- "I'm wondering if you'd be willing to introduce me to Ravi Chopra."
- "Ravi Chopra seems like such a cool guy, and he's doing really cool things, and I've read up on him, but there's no substitute for actually meeting someone, and you mentioned that the two of you were in business school together, so do you think that might work for me to have a conversation? I mean if it's okay with you. I don't know if he'd even be willing to meet with me, but you never know."

This is not an extreme example. I hear people doing this all the time. They end up bumbling because they haven't taken the time to come up with clear language. Or they are trying to soften their request. But clouding your message doesn't help anyone.

## Stay on Your Side of the Net

Try to avoid saying things like this:

- "I'd like a signing bonus, but I don't know if that's even possible."
- "We're requesting donations of $500, but we understand people are at different levels, so anything is appreciated."
- "I don't like negotiating with clients, so I start each proposal with a 10 percent discount."

My coaching colleague, Madelyn, frequently reminds me, "Stay on your side of the net." Staying on your side of the net means to stay focused on your own position, not the other side's. Get clear about it, put it forth, and wait for a response.

This might seem hard-edged, but it actually shows humility. To stay on your side of the net means that you believe the other person is capable, grounded, and able to negotiate for what they want.

# TWENTY-MINUTES-A-DAY EXERCISES

- **Exercise 1:** Ask your boss for a midyear check-in (outside the normal review process).
- **Exercise 2:** Ask someone to review an email you are going to send where you are trying to get the tone just right.
- **Exercise 3:** Stop by a party or event for twenty minutes, talk to three people, then leave.

# CHAPTER 12
# Persistence

Henry Robles grew up as one of ten children in a Pentecostal Mexican-American family in West Texas. A small kid with a big personality, Henry excelled in academics and was also a joiner—he did band, journalism, drama, you name it. He loved watching sports, a necessity when you grow up in Texas. He read constantly and enjoyed writing, and his teachers told him he was good at it.

He attended the honors program at the University of Texas at Austin, and he loved college. He was admitted to law school but deferred. For two years, he worked as a bilingual elementary school teacher in Los Angeles. Then he headed to law school. He planned to become a civil rights lawyer.

Henry didn't like law school. Studying law had a way of making people both competitive and boring. His grades were less than stellar, something he wasn't used to. But he'd acquired a credential and also a lot of debt. He still wanted to believe in the dream, so after graduation in 1996, he took a job with a litigation firm in Los Angeles.

Very quickly it became obvious that his real interests and talents were more on the creative side. Henry's true passion was playwriting, but he started to plot out a future in television writing. Henry spent four years at the law firm, paying down his debt, putting away savings, and trying to work on his plays and scripts. But the eighty-hour weeks of corporate law didn't allow enough time to make meaningful progress.

When he was ready, he quit his job, signed up with a temp agency, and started working as a contract lawyer at the same types of firms where he had previously been an associate. There was no status, and he worked at a desk in a hallway, but the hours were contained, and he still had income coming in. Most importantly, from 5 PM onwards, his time was his own.

Henry wrote and wrote. He networked. He applied for writing programs. But despite meeting people in the industry, he couldn't land an agent. He participated in a brand-new program for minority writers, but there was no connection to specific jobs afterwards. He kept on writing. He finished two plays and several spec scripts. He lived like a grad student in the same small apartment off Fairfax that he'd taken after graduation.

Through a fellow attorney, he met a man who was a building up his management business. He thought Henry had great potential. "I want to work with you. I'm going to pitch you as a lawyer from Texas who writes plays. It's gonna be great." Henry agreed but was not optimistic.

A few weeks later, Henry's new manager set up a meeting with an agent. They hit it off. In short order, four different talent agencies wanted to represent Henry. "We love your spec script," they said. "And we love your play."

Henry signed with one. A few months later, he was a staff writer on the show *Cold Case*. This was 2004, eight years after he'd graduated from law school and three-plus years after he'd started his pursuit of a writing job. Henry broke through on the basis of the same spec script he had written two years before. For at least two years he'd had the bona fides to be a Hollywood writer but couldn't make the right connections. Eventually, he did.

Henry Robles is now known and respected in the industry. He's worked as a writer and producer on numerous shows, including *Station 19*, *Switched at Birth*, *Selena: The Series*, and *Rebel*. Now the industry has plenty of recognition for this skilled, funny, articulate, well-educated, bilingual, Mexican-American writer from Texas. When he was starting out and trying to find a way in, not so much. During that long span, Henry needed persistence.

When it comes to activating your invisible network and achieving your goals, there is no substitute for persistence. Sometimes you'll find a quick reciprocal flow. But other times you are going to find yourself in the position where you are making efforts without getting much in return—at least nothing you can see. You will often need to stay on it and manage your own frustration while you wait for the right things to happen.

## Situations Requiring Persistence

Mastering your invisible network isn't searching for likes on Instagram. Don't expect instant gratification, and don't evaluate your success based on immediate feedback. There are three major challenges that require persistence.

First, you need to cultivate your network. A network is like a garden. You can plant your seeds and hope for the best, but you'll be more successful if you fertilize the soil, water regularly, check for weeds and pests, and add nutrients as necessary. You need to nurse things along and pay attention over time, even when you're not yet seeing results.

Second, you need to win other people's attention. Everyone is busy and focused on other things. You are disrupting a system. You are trying to shift someone's eye from something else to you.

Third, in certain fields you need to invest over the long run to get results. You may need to invest *years* of effort before achieving your results. I will give examples of these below.

## Dealing with Nonresponses and Keeping at It

I'm going to talk about dealing with nonresponses when you reach out to specific people with carefully crafted messages. I am *not* including in this discussion nonresponses when you apply online to the big internet black hole of job listings. You will *not* get very far in life by limiting your job searches to online applications. Whenever I hear someone complaining about how badly their job search is going because they applied to two hundred jobs online and didn't get any response, I want to shake them. That is not how you get jobs, and it's certainly not how you develop meaningful relationships.

Now that we have that clarification out the way, let's talk about how to deal with nonresponses.

You might be afraid of receiving a "no" to your request, but in my experience clear noes are somewhat unusual. You will often get a yes, or no response at all. Nonresponses are a big part of reaching out. Strangers don't respond, and close friends frequently don't respond either.

Let's look at a few scenarios:

- **Nonresponse.** You initiated a call or email, and nothing happened.
- **Response without an answer.** In this case, the person responds to your outreach but doesn't take up your suggestion to meet.
- **Consideration without commitment.** This takes the form of, "Let me check," or "Let think about it and see what I can do."

Not getting a response to your polite messages doesn't feel great. It can really take the wind out of your sails. But you need to get a hold of yourself. People are busy, they have competing commitments, and they forget things.

You can follow up in a manner that neither makes them feel guilty nor makes you an apologist for their inaction.

**Example One:**
Dear Jack,

I hope your week is going well. I wanted to check in on my email about finding time to get together. Does next week work for you?

—Michael

**Example Two:**

Dear Jack,

Just a ping. I'd love to get something on the calendar. Does next week work? I'm forwarding my original email, which provides background—I'd love to get your thoughts on NFTs and anything else.

–Michael

Avoid being needy ("I really don't know who else to ask"), whiny ("I'm surprised you haven't answered"), or defensive ("I'm really sorry to keep bothering you"). Also be careful about humor ("I guess someone has had some late nights!") unless you are certain it will land well—it's easy to misinterpret, and it can sound overfamiliar.

▲▼▲

Being persistent requires you to manage your thoughts, feelings, and energy. Let's look at some ways to do this.

## Focus on General Responsiveness, Not Specific Responsiveness

You won't always get what you ask for. A better goal is to *generally* get what you want from your network as a whole, not to get what you want from each person in your life. Come up with a desired percentage. I'd recommend 20 or 30 percent. If you get what you want 30 percent of the times you ask for it, you're doing well.

## Check Your Perspectives

Before you reach dark conclusions about why someone is not getting back to you, check your perspectives and assumptions.

Here's a self-coaching tool I've used hundreds of times in the past twenty years: the perspectives wheel. (We're using it to analyze this specific frustration, but you can use it for any situation where you're feeling stuck or confused.)

Start by drawing a large circle on a piece of paper, then divide it into eight even pizza slices. These are going to be your perspectives.

Define the issue: "I've sent Joe three messages, and he hasn't gotten back to me," or "I asked my best friend to help move, and she said she's busy," or "I've gone to ten networking events in my field and haven't developed any business."

You then write your first interpretation of this situation. When you are frustrated, these are often negative: "No one wants to help me," or "He's sending me the message that he doesn't want to talk to me," or "These events are a waste of time."

Push yourself to come up with a second view on the matter. "People have been coming to these events for years; I just started three months ago," or "All my friends are moms with young children and have a lot on their minds," or "He's really established and might get twenty requests like mine each week."

Continue along until you have eight different interpretations of the same situation. By the time you get to perspectives six, seven, and eight, you are really pushing your brain into new territory.

Then read each one. Decide which two or three feel most right to you. Then pick the perspective that is *most useful* for you to have. Based on this perspective, what are your next steps?

I tried this when I experienced some frustration around reaching out to a former client, Rishi. We had worked together for six months, with positive results. We had a lot in common: We went to the same college, both had twin sons, and lived two blocks away from each other. He is Indian American, and I had lived in India for a year when I was younger.

After our coaching engagement concluded, I was looking forward to being friends. I invited him to have lunch a few times and also suggested we get our kids together as well. But I got no uptake. He was busy on particular dates and never returned the bid. I felt he didn't want to become friends, which was confusing because the fundamentals were there.

I tried the perspectives wheel exercise.

My first perspective was: "Rishi doesn't understand how relationships work or what bids are."

My second perspective was: "He's super busy. Both he and his wife work, and their kids are in an intense school. He can't find the time."

I added more: "A coaching client relationship is different from a friendship, and you can't always make the transition." I also wrote, "Maybe his wife determines his social calendar."

Here's what my circle looked like in the end:

## Perspectives Wheel—Rishi Isn't Responding to My Invitations

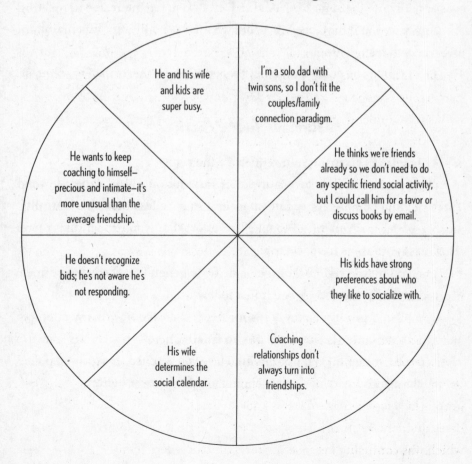

He and his wife and kids are super busy.

I'm a solo dad with twin sons, so I don't fit the couples/family connection paradigm.

He wants to keep coaching to himself—precious and intimate—it's more unusual than the average friendship.

He thinks we're friends already so we don't need to do any specific friend social activity; but I could call him for a favor or discuss books by email.

He doesn't recognize bids; he's not aware he's not responding.

His kids have strong preferences about who they like to socialize with.

His wife determines the social calendar.

Coaching relationships don't always turn into friendships.

All of these could have been true. But when I read it, I decided the perspective about, "We're friends already and don't need to do any specific friend social activity" sounded most true. Plus, I was sure he was indeed busy and finding ninety minutes for lunch or two hours for a family visit can be incredibly hard.

Oddly, Rishi reached out to me just after I wrote the first draft of this chapter. I'd sent him a holiday card, and he wrote back an email suggesting coffee. We caught up, and I asked him about his nonresponse.

He said, "It's possible I didn't recognize the bid. But the real reason is getting my family organized to do anything has a high cost. Seeing you is easy, but getting my wife and kids along is a major undertaking."

What I thought would be easy—"Hey, let's get our families together!"— was actually very hard for him. And in fact, I wasn't *so* interested in meeting his family. It would have been nice, but what I was really after was maintaining our own friendship.

I was right to be persistent. I just needed to adjust the form of my request.

## Review Your Practices

Check whether you made your request in the right way.

My rule of thumb is to assume a 3:1 ratio for outreach. Expect to send three outgoing emails for each response. It may be less than this in reality, but it's better for something to take less effort than you expect than more. How many attempts have you made?

Did you hit the right balance of specific to general, or direct to indirect? Consider modifying the approach in a follow-up.

Establish a give-up policy. This means you decide how many attempts you will make before giving up (e.g., two emails and one text, or three invitations, or one voicemail and one email). Have you reached this give-up point? If not, try again. If yes, shift your energy to other network efforts.

## Some Network Building Is Hard

There are certain situations where success will take much more investment on your part. Some types of network building can be harder than average for several specific reasons:

- The field is highly competitive
- You need credibility, but can only build it over time
- The field requires extreme focus to develop technical skills, leaving very little time for relationship building
- You're expected to show your mettle by your persistence—it's seen as your job to keep trying
- The key players are not obvious, or they are constantly changing
- It's clear who the key players are, but it's difficult to get their attention

Let's look more deeply at two types of hard relationship-building situations.

### (1) When It's Your Job to Keep It Going

Venture capitalists meet people all the time. They are constantly networking. They compete with one another to find ways to invest the money they've spent. A VC may spend several hours a day meeting company founders.

This doesn't mean the founders have it easy. If you're looking for investors to put money into your company, it's your job to find them and make your case. One email will not suffice. When you don't get a response, you have to keep trying.

"If someone gave up trying to meet me after three attempts, I would question whether they have what it takes to make a company successful," one investor told me. "I'm not deliberately trying to be nonresponsive. But I'm busy, and I expect them to be able to break through the noise."

Finding investors is one of the *easiest* parts of building a successful company. Much harder are the challenges of building an innovative product, hiring, leading the team, fighting the competition, and making a profit. If you're tempted to give up because potential investors aren't responding to your inquiries, you probably don't have the grit required to build a company.

Some fields are extremely competitive to enter or to rise in. Most people won't make it, so established players expect people who are going to make it to push themselves forward. Examples are:

- Politics and elected office
- Acting, music, and performing arts
- Journalism and writing
- Publishing
- Television writing and screenwriting
- Television and film production
- Academia (tenured positions and/or desirable locations)
- Investment banking
- Private equity/venture capital
- Any kind of entrepreneurship

When my client Lauren Baer ran for Congress, it was her first run at elected office. She won her primary but not the general. There's a strong incumbency advantage in U.S. politics, and I asked how she dealt with the likelihood of losing. She said, "It's hard to win, and it's hard to win as a first-time candidate. Many of our elected leaders in office right now didn't win the first time that they ran for office. It was a process of running, losing, learning, and building support over time. If you're so risk-averse that you're not going to enter an election unless you know that winning is the definitive outcome, politics probably isn't for you, and you're probably not in it for the right reasons."

## (2) When Success Takes a Long Time

In other areas, it can take a long time to see career or financial benefits from a relationship. This shows up particularly in sales, business development, and fundraising. Law, accounting, financial services, and management consulting all have a sales component. Nonprofit organizations must be competent in sales: it's called development. You might be a global expert on public health, but if you can't raise money from institutional donors and governments, you won't rise to the top in a large NGO.

A sales trainer once taught me that there are two key moments in a sales cycle: The first moment is when you educate the client about your offering. This is when they learn what you do and understand how your services could benefit them. The second moment is when the client is ready to buy something—when they have the need.

This is the hard thing about sales: you may have already created a wonderful impression for a client, yet they may forget to think about you at the most crucial moment. The implication is that you may need to nurture a relationship for a long time before you see financial results.

## Managing Yourself in a Long-Term Effort

When you're engaged in long-term or otherwise challenging network development, the most important thing is to keep up your own efforts, energy, and spirit. The basic problem in these situations is that you are not getting positive feedback on a regular basis. The solution to this is to design your own measurement system. Instead of waiting for the world to validate your efforts, you are going to have to validate them yourself.

You validate and manage your own efforts by having three things:

1. Measurement of inputs
2. A method of learning by doing and course correction
3. An overall faith in your effort

## Measurement of Inputs

Instead of measuring outputs, measure inputs. These are under your control. When I coach lawyers, financiers, and consultants in business development, I suggest they decide on the number of outreach conversations they are going to have—say, thirty over a period of six months. They then track back to figure out how many outgoing emails or calls they need to set these up. For a busy person, this is not an overwhelming number—a bit more than once a week—but it still takes conscious effort.

Input variables you can measure are:

- Email outreach
- Conversations
- Companies or organizations you make connections at
- Proposals
- Events you attend (or hold)
- Publications you author
- LinkedIn comments you make
- LinkedIn connections
- Research on particular people or sectors
- Twenty-minute segments you spend on any of the above

Ground yourself in a realistic idea of how long something will take or how hard it is. Ask people who are knowledgeable how long things take. I tell new coaches that when they hit five hundred hours of direct service, they will jump into another level of competence and client demand. They are a bit shocked by this (most training programs require less than fifty hours of coaching) and at the same time reassured that *something* will eventually happen.

If you're in a highly competitive field with high barriers to entry, don't ask for reassurance. Ask for hardheaded wisdom.

## A Method of Learning by Doing and Course Correction

Feedback is an indispensable part of learning. Absent direct feedback from others, you can still build a habit of assessing your efforts. Use a simple series of questions to audit how you are doing. For example, after each networking conversation, ask yourself:

1.  What went well?
2.  What didn't go as well?
3.  How would I rate this conversation on a 1 to 10 scale? Why?
4.  How would I rate my own performance on a 1 to 10 scale? Why do I give myself this score?
5.  If I were to do this again, what would I do differently?

Example: Andre evaluates a conversation he had with Sharice. Andre works in the office of his local congressman and is trying to figure out how to move up. Sharice is someone with twenty years' experience on Capitol Hill.

1.  What went well?
    *She responded to my inquiry and took the time to meet even though we have a weak connection. I prepared questions, and she answered them.*
2.  What didn't go as well?
    *The questions I asked were not very interesting. I could have asked her more interesting things had I prepared more thoughtfully.*
3.  How would I rate this conversation on a 1 to 10 scale? Why?
    *Seven out of ten. The convo itself was not very useful, but now I am connected to a significant person. She also gave me two names to follow up with.*
4.  How would I rate my own performance on a 1 to 10 scale? Why do I give myself this score?

*Five out of ten. I'm disappointed in myself for not putting more thought into my preparation. On the other hand, I think she will remember me as professional and polite. I don't think she would have given me the names if I came off badly. But I want to be more memorable! Not just another random D.C. staffer!*

5.  If I were to do this again, what would I do differently?
    *Ask two or three friends what types of questions would be useful for someone of Sharice's caliber. I spent a lot of effort making this connection; it wouldn't take much more time to be better prepared.*

## An Overall Faith in Your Effort

When I entered college, I had dreams of writing for the *Harvard Lampoon.* I was funny! And what could be more fun than hanging with other funny people?

At Harvard, you have to compete, or "comp," to do most extracurriculars. I wrote several sketches and showed up for the informational session for the comp, which was held in the Lampoon's castle, an actual castle-type building off Massachusetts Avenue. There were tons of people there, and you could feel the excited vibrations.

A few Lampoon guys gave their spiel: They wrote issues of the magazine, then sold them nationally and made tons of money, and with the proceeds had blow-out dinners in their castle. A feature of the dinners was to take all the dinner china and glasses and fling them against the walls of the castle. "How cool is that?" the main guy said. Everyone laughed hearing about these hilarious, crazy antics.

The whole thing grossed me out. I hadn't anticipated that writing comedy would require me to participate in this stupid bro culture. I felt my enthusiasm drain out of my body. I went back to my dorm and never returned to the Lampoon again. (I'll tell you who didn't slink off to his dorm: Conan O'Brien, who was in my college class and in all likelihood was at that same meeting.)

Looking back, I don't know if the Lampoon or comedy was for me, but I do know that I sold myself out that night. I took my feelings too seriously. I gave the preppie Lampoon bros, who most likely were just cocky, insecure, socially challenged college guys, all my power. I lacked faith in my effort, or perhaps it just didn't occur to me that my self-belief was more important than what anyone else said and more important than the discomfort I was feeling. I could have had more faith in my ambition.

You're the leader of your own life. It might be nice to have others cheering you along, but in the end, you'll need to be your biggest cheerleader. So take responsibility for self-belief.

In addition to setting goals, you can to lean into "identify formation." Identity formation includes the idea that your future actions depend on how you define your identity. For example, if no one from your family or community has ever gone to college, it's helpful to say, "My goal is to graduate from college," but it's even more helpful if you believe, "I'm the kind of person who will graduate from college."

Identity formation is easier when you see people like yourself achieving similar goals. This is one reason why diversity in all respects is important. (I'd contemplated parenthood for decades, but what finally pushed me into action was receiving a text from Adam, a gay high school friend who'd just become a father through surrogacy and IVF. *If he did it, then I'm going to do it.*)

You can will yourself into a type of identity formation. This means that you *define yourself as the kind of person who is successful in this goal.* You don't have to fully believe this; half-believing it is enough if you're willing to keep at it.

Examples of identity-formation statements for going after tough goals are:

- "I'm the kind of person who succeeds at hard things."
- "I'm the kind of person who doesn't give up after disappointment or setbacks."
- "I'm the kind of person who breaks through every barrier."

- "I'm the kind of person who belongs in the C-suite."
- "I'm the kind of person who will buy her parents a house."
- "I'm the kind of person who is made for the Lampoon."

## Exercise: When I'm Old (or When I'm Successful)

Imagine yourself in the future, looking back on you at this age. Imagine that this future, older, more successful you is grateful for and pleased about what you are doing right now. Write five sentences about why.

Example: *"When I'm old, I'll look back at this time and be proud that I managed to write a whole book while raising two young kids."*

Example: *"When I'm successful, I'll look back at myself and be grateful that I looked at every failure as an opportunity to learn how to get better."*

1. _____
2. _____
3. _____
4. _____
5. _____

## Ramp Up the Stakes

A final technique when dealing with something hard, or when you feel stuck, is to ramp up the stakes. Make your goals bigger, harder, and more exciting. See what you can dare yourself to do. If you're trying to meet an SVP, try to meet the CEO. If you're going to attend a conference, submit a proposal to be a panelist.

When I heard that my former client was running for Congress, I said, "I'll host a fundraiser for you at my apartment."

I made Lauren this offer notwithstanding the general ineptness of my prior efforts at fundraising. However, once I realized that I was inviting people to my own apartment to raise money for someone I personally cared about, I knew that failure was not an option. I signed up two friends as cohosts, and we schemed how we were going to make this event successful.

As I set things up, I marveled at how much more aggressive I had become and more consistent in my follow-through. I wrote to people, I continually added to the list, and I tracked everything on a constantly updated spreadsheet. As the day approached, I made sure to keep guests pinned down. "Looking forward to seeing you tomorrow night!" I'd text. And then day of: "Can't wait to see you in a few hours." If they were going to flake out, it would not go unnoticed!

The event was a great success. It gathered a different mix of people than I'd previously experienced and, in line with the principles of this book, I wouldn't have been able to predict who would show up. We had political people and lawyers, neighbors, and also people I would never have imagined might attend.

## TWENTY-MINUTES-A-DAY EXERCISES

- **Exercise 1:** Write five identity-formation statements related to one of your big goals.
- **Exercise 2:** Review the "Measurement of Inputs" section in this chapter. Decide which input(s) you want to use. Create a simple tracker to capture this for the next few weeks.
- **Exercise 3:** Revise your Relationship Portfolio Bingo Card for the next month.

# CHAPTER 13
# Exercising Your Convening Power

As a kid, I was not a club person. I *wanted* to be a club person, but I couldn't seem to make it happen. I wasn't good at team sports. I was semi-respected but not popular. And I assumed correctly that my natural interests—drama, music, singing, reading—were not the sorts of things that would establish me socially. I was known as smart and some-times as a smart aleck, neither of which led to a sense of belonging. I was desperate to be liked yet simultaneously looked down on a lot of my class-mates. I was part of the debate "team," but this consisted of my partner—Robyn—and myself. I did occasionally join things, but when I'd show up to a club meeting, I felt I was playacting. Decades later, I can summon the feel-ing I'd have arriving at a meeting, information session, or party: awkward-ness, shifting my weight from foot to foot, trying to figure out how to enter the conversation. I never, ever would have used the word *leader* to describe myself. It never occurred to me that my feelings might have something to do with adolescence.

When I was twenty-two, my roommates and I decided to have a big party for my birthday. I was an apprentice teacher in the English as a Second

Language program at Harvard Summer School, and I'd met a crowd of witty, very verbal, countercultural, globe-trotting ESL teachers. My roommates and I invited them to our party, along with international students, friends, and random people we had met that week. The party was a wild success. It was at that point that I realized I didn't have to become a different type of person to bring people together. I could just set up an event and invite people.

To use a phrase I'm sure I'd never heard, I actually had convening power. And you have it, too. You just have to exercise it.

To get the full power of your invisible network, you need to get beyond one-on-one interactions. Convening others strengthens your invisible network in two ways. First, it allows you to interact with more people and with many people at the same time. Second, it allows you to facilitate connections among other people. This is good for them, and it also benefits you. The more you make convening a habit, the easier it will be.

Convening is another example of compounding interest. The benefit is logarithmic, not arithmetic. Impact multiplies.

## Why Convene?

Groups organized for a particular purpose have value beyond that purpose. It's a modern cliché that people in book clubs often don't read the books. But that doesn't matter. If a group of friends or readers are getting together from time to time, that creates social capital. I used to think that school fundraisers like auctions and carnivals were inefficient. Wouldn't you raise more money if the people involved just worked longer hours and wrote checks representing part of those wages? But by soliciting items and reaching out to merchants and reminding parents and having tons of planning meetings, the folks on those committees are learning about each other, building trust, and building relationships, some of which will last far longer than the events. This is also why attending a charitable event is a positive action, even if you know nothing about the charity or would be willing to make a donation without attending.

Happiness expert Gretchen Rubin has noted that people are happier in groups. Groups provide members with a sense of belonging and joy, facilitate the transmission of important information, and contribute to personal development. Rubin says you can join a group or create one yourself. You may not even realize you are creating a group when you do it. I know many groups of women who first met in college or graduate school and who continue to meet decades later, keeping in touch, planning girls' trips, and being strong ties for each other.

In chapter three, I quoted television writer Elizabeth Craft, who says that people become successful in groups. Everyone ages at the same rate, regardless of your starting points, so you are all accumulating experiences and connections and gathering wisdom. The group creates a basis of trust and an easy way to reconnect. If you're in a good group, you might be dragged along to success.

Like-minded groups allow people to share common interests and questions that they might otherwise just experience individually. Before I became a coach, I was a lawyer (among other things). I didn't consider myself a lawyer's lawyer, but that mode of thinking and those experiences do influence how I see the world. As it happens, there are many coaches who are also lawyers. In my view, lawyer coaches have more emotional intelligence than most lawyers and stronger critical thinking skills than most coaches. Conversation flows very easily when we are together.

If you build it, they will probably come. People are attracted to quality people and quality interactions. Once I realized that I had the power to convene people, I started hosting more parties and dinners. These ebb and flow depending on the year, but I would say the two brand attributes of any party I have will be (1) the food will be good and plentiful, and (2) you will meet quality people.

A group can be tightly defined or loose, but once it gets going, it tends to keep its own dynamic. You may be the initiator, but other people can take a role in keeping it going.

## Ways to Convene

There are lots of different ways you can exercise your convening power. Examples are:

- Organize or be part of teams, groups, committees, clubs, and organizations
- Take on a predesigned role, like class agent for a college, or a member of a school committee
- Host dinner parties and brunches
- Form a trio or small group with friends and agree to meet from time to time

It's not just people who convene things. Organizations and companies can do this as well. For instance, the Rockefeller Foundation is a major philanthropic organization that gives out more than $170 million each year in grants. But it also sees part of its power as being a convening force—it has the ability to get a lot of interesting and significant people in a room. It can draw attention to issues that are beyond the scope of its own grantmaking.

You can often convene groups as part of work. Most large companies have employee resource groups (ERGs) on one topic or another, and the topics are always evolving. You can show up or you can take on a leadership role. The positive thing about a specific role is that it gives you a justification for connecting with people you don't know very well—you're doing a job. Many professional groups are poorly run and don't reach anything near their potential, so if you're willing to put in some time and energy, you can make a difference, and you will probably get noticed.

## Examples of Groups

- I have a friendship with Marci Alboher and Gretchen Rubin, lawyers-turned-writers I met more than fifteen years ago. From the time we met, our conversations had great energy, and we decided to continue meeting regularly. We called it MGM after the first initials of our names. We started meeting every six weeks or so, and now connect twice a year, including a meeting around Christmas each year where we do an annual goal-setting exercise.

- Faith Adiele is a writer who has taught courses on creative nonfiction and memoir at the college and graduate level for many years. Her world included people who were versed in literature from multiple ethnic groups, including Black American and Caribbean writers, but there was little discussion of African literature. Faith grew up in the U.S., but her father was Nigerian and she had spent time in Africa. She started her African literature book club to help introduce people to existing and emerging writers, and the group has met regularly for several years.

- Colin Carroll practiced law in Ireland and England for a few years. He left the practice of law but remained interested in the lives of lawyers. He zeroed in on the great discomfort most lawyers seemed to feel in business development. He started the Lawyers' Business Development Club in 2011. The concept was to invite noteworthy guests to address an audience of lawyers. The lawyers would want to hear what the speakers had to say, and the speakers would enjoy having an audience that someone else organized. It turned out that the platform was enough to get top authors, in-house counsel, and business leaders, such as the chairman of Goldman Sachs International, the CEO of O2 (UK), and the CEO of Facebook (Ireland), to come give talks, and it turned out that reticent lawyers really enjoyed coming to these events. The events grew as guest speakers introduced Colin to other guest speakers, and over time Colin ran talks not just in London and Dublin but also Paris, Dubai, Boston, New York, and San Francisco.

## How to Get a Group Going

There are many ways you can approach this.

- **Topic versus people.** You can pick a subject or demographic you are personally interested in. What's the group you wish existed? Alternately, you can identify people you'd like to hang out with and survey them to see what the basis of the group would be.

- **New versus existing.** You can create a brand-new group. Alternately, you could take a leadership role in another group that is successful or languishing. It takes effort to run groups, so there might be successful group leaders who are ready to turn over the reins.

- **Pilot event versus planned series.** You can start with just one event—a pilot—and see how it goes. Alternately, you can commit yourself to a series of events—say four, six, or ten meetings during the year. People may have lots of interest but not be able to make the first or second meeting.

- **Tight-knit versus open enrollment.** You can start small and committed—three or four people you can count on. You can wait until things feel solid before opening it up. Alternately, you can start bigger and looser: invite a bunch of people, see who shows up, and be open to the direction their energy takes.

- **No commitment versus skin in the game.** There are times when you want to make things as easy as possible for potential joiners— you don't want to create unnecessary barriers to entry. On the other hand, you might want people to have skin in the game—they need to commit or contribute something. You could require people to bring something to eat or drink, fill out a questionnaire ahead of time, or be prepared to share something specific. In my experience, the more you demand of people, the more they respect the experience.

## Managing Your Own Motivation

Exercising your convening power means you are taking things up a notch. With greater effort comes greater risk of disappointment. Here are some tips for managing this:

1. **Remember that you don't control everything.** Some groups take off, and some don't. Maybe this particular group just doesn't want to happen, even if people have said they would love to attend. It's okay to let it go. You can try something else later.

2. **Be realistic about how much time you have to invest.** Don't commit yourself to something that is going to irritate you or make you feel you are underperforming. In general, fewer meetings are better. If you think something should be monthly, consider whether it should be quarterly. Even two meetings a year can accomplish a lot.

3. **Articulate clearly what the benefit *to you* is.** Are you finding a way to connect with friends, trying out a leadership role, or serving a cause you believe in? There's something in it for you, and you should know what it is. You're going to be spending a fair amount of time sending out emails, dealing with people's schedules, and reminding people of things they should have remembered from the first time you told them. The more you remember what's in it for you, the less annoyed or frustrated you'll get.

4. **Ask for help.** Others may not want the central organizing role, but they may be happy to help. People enjoy being successful in clearly defined tasks, so do some delegating.

## TWENTY-MINUTES-A-DAY EXERCISES————————————

- **Exercise 1:** At the end of your next meeting, spend five to ten minutes taking stock of what has been accomplished. Questions you could ask: "How effective has this meeting been for us?" "What has been the best part of this meeting?" "What would we do differently next time?"

- **Exercise 2:** According to Priya Parker, author of *The Art of Gathering: How We Meet and Why It Matters*, the start and end of events are opportunities for great impact. You can grab people's attention or provide a sense of closure and meaning. She advises not starting or ending group events with comments about logistics ("Your folders are on the back table" or "The buses will be leaving for the dinner at 6:30 PM") or by saying, "Thank you." (She says that "thank you" can be the second-to-last thing, but shouldn't be the last thing.) With that in mind, write out how you will start or end your next meeting or group event.

- **Exercise 3:** Plan a potluck dinner or informal brunch. In your invitation, say, "I want to make this more of a habit, and this will be the kickoff event."

# PART 4
# Special Kinds of Relationships

# CHAPTER 14
# Finding Mentors and Turning Mentors into Sponsors

B arack Obama is an amazing person, but he didn't get where he did by himself. Early on, a Chicago mover and shaker named Valerie Jarrett took notice of him. She recognized his ambition, capabilities, and potential. Five years his senior and more experienced in Chicago politics and industry than he was, Jarrett gave Obama advice, made introductions, and kept an eye on him. She continued to play this role through his campaigns and during both terms of his presidency.

Sheryl Sandberg is also an amazing person, but she didn't get where she did by herself either. As a college student, she got to know Larry Summers, first a noted economics professor with connections throughout the political world and later secretary of the treasury and president of Harvard. As a young woman, Sandberg impressed him, and she worked by his side for years in government. He then facilitated her introduction to Silicon Valley, which at the time was far more interested in engineers than in business generalists. She entered a senior position at Google and ultimately became the number two at Facebook.

Both Obama and Sandberg had sponsors. A sponsor is someone who acts on your behalf, makes a case for you, and persuades others in support of you. Sponsors are rare and powerful and worth looking for.

Mentors are on the same relationship continuum but somewhat different. A mentor is someone who shares wisdom, gives you guidance, and helps you develop. A mentor is interested in your development, though not making an intervention with others on your behalf.

People are very intrigued about the idea of mentors and sponsors. Having them seems like a fast track to success. They also seem like resources that are unfairly distributed in the world. Do some people get all the good ones? Do some people get set up with them because of family connections or unfair advantages? What are my options if I'm "different"?

Mentors and sponsors are special relationships, but they are also normal relationships. It's in your power to develop them. This includes three separate tasks:

1. Looking for them
2. Being appropriately receptive when they come along
3. Forwarding and deepening the relationship(s) when they come into your life

Sometimes these relationships are beyond reach, but sometimes they are right in front of you, waiting for you to open your eyes and get out of your own way.

## The Continuum of Concern and Helping

Mentor and sponsor are not wholly distinct categories. There is a continuum of how people engage with you, and a person can move from one to another. Consider the following stages of how a professional contact may show up in your life.

- Stranger
- Networking contact (weak tie)
- Networking contact (better known)
- Mentor
- Sponsor

These identities can overlap with others: friend, colleague, fellow committee member, boss, and so on.

This is important because people get hung up on sponsors. That's going from zero to sixty fast. Most mentor and sponsor relationships show up as something else first.

Niki Khoshzamir immigrated from Iran to attend college and law school in the U.S. She later started a company called PracticePro that helps prepare law students and new lawyers—in particular first-generation professionals and students from underrepresented minority backgrounds—to be successful in the professional world. Her company aims to equip them with the more mysterious skills about professional advancement that law schools don't teach.

Mentors and sponsors are part of this. But as she told me in a podcast interview, these are normal relationships and it's not useful to think of them as strictly different categories. The first time you meet a future mentor or sponsor, he or she may simply seem like someone you're drawn to.

Mentors are people that you want to be like because they're amazing professionals, or you see that they have four kids and they're a partner at a firm. It could be someone with great work/life balance. It could be someone who has exceptional skills.

It's not always about how they can help you get things. When I talk to my mentors, I could just tell them about me. "This is what I'm thinking right now. This is what I'm worried about right now." Their advice may be more important than any connections they might make. A mentor isn't necessarily a lower category than a sponsor or advocate. It's about the person, not the category. Over time you start recognizing who is an outstanding mentor or sponsor for you, based on how the relationship is working for you.

In terms of finding them, it's a step-by-step process. I don't look up and say, "Michael has this perfect thing. I'm going to go befriend him and ask him to be my sponsor." Because that might violate the principles of good networking, which is connecting with people, keeping in touch with them, and then just seeing how organically this relationship grows.

Whatever is drawing you, you approach these people, have a conversation with them, keep in touch with them, and then ask them questions. And eventually you might make requests of them. I'll be like, "Hey, Michael, I'm really interested in genomics. Do you know somebody?"

## Case Study: Helping Veronica

Around the time I started coaching, I had a one-man test prep business. I hired a person named Dan the Flyer Man to put up flyers on the Upper West Side advertising my offering. One of my first calls was a high school senior named Veronica, who was going to take the SAT. We did some intensive prep, and I learned that her father was a handyman in a large apartment building and that her mother was a homemaker, her family of four lived in a one-bedroom apartment, and she had been on full scholarship at a nearby private school her whole life. In other words, she was not going to be a big-money, rich-kid client. On the other hand, she was the kind of person I knew I wanted to help. She and her family had very little idea how selective college admissions work, but I knew this system very well. I'd cracked it when I was in high school and added to my knowledge in college and grad school. I knew exactly how to play this game, and I wanted her to benefit from this hard-won knowledge.

By the time we moved on from the SAT to the actual applications, this was a volunteer gig on my part. I helped her understand how to position herself. I told her, "What highly selective colleges love are working-class minority students with strong survival skills." She ran with it because, in fact, she had amazing resilience and a great story to tell. We met for many hours in Starbucks on 86th and Columbus—she applied to thirteen schools. So you can say I was a close-up mentor at this time. I didn't introduce her to anyone, but I gave her my opinion about which elements of her background schools would find interesting, and which of her initial essay ideas were intriguing or ho-hum.

Veronica ended up going to Georgetown, which she loved. It was not without its challenges. We'd check in from time to time, and I'd ask how things were going. I'm sure I gave a lot of general advice. It probably included things like, "Meet your professors and let them get to know you" and "Walk into the financial aid office and say you need more" and "You're allowed to drop a class if you aren't doing well. Forget your pride." I drew on my own life experience as well as that of my mom, dad, sisters, and classmates.

We stayed in touch as she entered her first professional job. I had some concerns—I hadn't heard of the company; it was in a random part of New Jersey; and it seemed sketchy. I knew that your career could stall out for years in the wrong job. Within a year or two she had become frustrated.

She'd applied online for an opening at a magazine she liked, but she didn't get an interview. I had an acquaintance from business school who was CEO of a magazine in the portfolio of the same holding company, someone who was from an adjoining circle. I shifted into a new mode of helping: I wrote a polite email to my contact, titled "Excellent diversity candidate worth a look?" I was very careful with my tone: "No obligation of course, but this may be the type of person one of your companies is interested in." Within a few days, she had an interview, we prepped for it, and eventually she got a job with the *People*-branded magazine family.

Reaching out to put in a word or make a connection is a sponsor move. I didn't get her a job—she did that herself. And my contact didn't arrange an interview to make me happy—he did it because he, like all executives, is always on the lookout for talent and knows that it can come through all kinds of channels. If she wasn't the right match, he could simply have sent a polite "no" or asked one of his colleagues to.

Here's the way my sponsorship did make a difference: my contact gets hundreds of emails a day, and it was more likely he'd read one that had his B-school classmate's name on it. He would also trust that I wouldn't recommend someone who did not have the bona fides—I have my own reputation to keep up, after all.

The interesting thing is that even after writing this passage, I would still consider Veronica as a friend, whereas I'm sure that she considers me as a mentor. Her family is very religious, and her mother once shared her belief that I'd been sent by God to help her daughter. I like this interpretation, not because I regard myself as an angel, but because seeing myself as a vessel for providing useful service is interesting. It takes the ego out of things. It's not about, *What is the amazing thing I'm going to do?* but instead, *The two of us are put together to do something great. Let's figure it out.* It's contemplating, *What is the mentoring relationship that wants to happen here?* There can be great benefit in having a mentor, and there can be great joy in being one.

## Mentors Versus Sponsors: How Much of a Difference Is There, Really?

Both roles support you. Let's compare how they do it:

| Mentor | Sponsor |
|---|---|
| • Listen<br>• Share experiences and wisdom<br>• Give feedback<br>• Give guidance and advice<br>• Give you tough love | • Make connections<br>• Write recommendations<br>• Offer judgment/approval in selection processes<br>• Use personal capital<br>• Give you tough love |

Sponsorship might seem more advanced than mentorship, but you can find instances of sponsorship in everyday life. If someone writes to another person introducing you and suggesting a get-together, they are sponsoring you: pinning their reputations to the idea that you are worth meeting. Setting up a blind date for two people is a kind of sponsorship. The teacher who wrote you a letter of recommendation for college was sponsoring you.

There's a type of sponsorship where someone *exercises power*, and this is the kind that people get excited about. It's sort of like having a tough older brother or sister. "You'd better take this person, or else." While I've seen a handful of examples of this, I don't think the world generally works this way. Sponsors play the biggest role not so much in *ordering* people to do things, but in *interpreting* things for them. Even when sponsors are pushing strongly for someone—for example in the partner selection process in consulting or banking—they are pushing a particular narrative: "Here's the reason why Ronald is the best candidate in the pool."

The other twist on sponsorship is that sponsors are implicated by what *you* do. If they support you and you are incompetent, create problems, or have a bad attitude, you are reflecting poorly on them, and you will diminish their capital going forward. That's another reason sponsors want to support capable people: even the most powerful or power-mad sponsors don't want to look bad because of what their protégés do.

Typically, mentors and sponsors are older than you, although this is not an ironclad rule. The more important qualifier is their level of experience and their position in relevant networks. You could have a sponsor close to your age or even younger. For instance, many people get into executive coaching after lengthy careers. Even though I've been doing this for a long time, newer coaches are often older than I am. I'm still in a place to potentially mentor and sponsor them.

Other fields, like technology and television writing, are very youth-centric. It's common to find young people in important roles.

## How You Do It: Keeping an Eye Out and Doing the Work

You form a relationship with a potential mentor or sponsor the same way you would with anyone else. The difference is that as you are creating relationships, you have an eye out for someone who might be able to help you advance in your career. It's a kind of Spidey sense that is good to develop. You are looking for someone with something to offer where there is some type of potential interest.

A first step is creatively thinking about what you might want—coming up with an image of what your potential mentors or sponsors might do for you and what they might look like.

## Exercise: Mentor/Sponsor Characteristics

You're more likely to find a mentor or sponsor when you have an idea what you are looking for. Answer the following questions to get clearer about the kind of person you'd like to know.

1. A question I have about my career is _____
   _____

2. Some expertise I'd benefit from is _____
   _____

3. I would learn a lot from a mentor who is around _____ years old. This is because _____

4. I'd love someone to introduce me to _____
   _____

5. The kinds of opportunities that I'd like someone to help me find are
   _____

6. I'd learn a lot from someone of the same gender/ethnic background as myself because _____
   _____

7. I'd learn a lot from someone who is from a different gender/ethnic background from myself because _____

8. A way I'd show appreciation to a mentor or sponsor is _____
   _____

## Are Your Eyes Open?

People assume that once a would-be mentor or sponsor appears in their lives, the job is done. But that's not true—it's not always obvious what is going on, and therefore you can screw up the mentor/sponsor enrollment process.

When I was in my training period in Washington, D.C., with the Foreign Service, I became friendly with an older colleague based in Washington, D.C. He was originally from Burma, was related to the former secretary general of the U.N., and had exquisite manners. We talked about working for the government, about Southeast Asia, about my study of Mandarin Chinese in college, about my upcoming assignment to Kolkata.

One day he said, "My wife and I have an extra ticket to see *Les Misérables* at the Kennedy Center this Friday. Would you like to come as our guest?"

I remember that moment very clearly. It was very hot that summer. I had a new boyfriend whom I was spending a lot of time with. And I remember thinking that *Les Misérables* might be kind of boring. "Oh—no, thanks," I said.

If I could go back in time, I would go back and slap myself! I answered this colleague's invitation—his bid—as if it were any random person asking me about my weekend plans. This was someone I could really learn from, who was likely very well connected and who really understood me. He was basically saying, "I'd like to welcome you into my world." And I said, "Oh—no, thanks."

A few years later I repeated the lameness. By then I was a summer associate at a major law firm. I met a number of senior associates—lawyers who were a year or two below partner promotion time—who were not much older than I was but were far ahead of me in their careers since they had gone straight through on their professional path whereas I'd worked in other jobs for several years. I enjoyed chatting from time to time with one of them—Edward. We also had a shared interest in Asia, and he himself was half-Korean. One detail stands out. I was asking a question about salaries, and he took a pencil and wrote down on a piece of yellow-ruled paper what the salaries were for each level of seniority. It was useful information. Almost any lawyer at the firm could have told me this, but no one had.

When I became a full-time lawyer at the firm after graduating from law school, we continued having limited but friendly contact. One day he left me a message. He and his wife were going to the opera that weekend and had an extra ticket. Would I like to go with them?

Reader, how do you think I responded? "Thanks for asking, but no thanks." Looking back, I would say to my younger self, "Seriously?"

I was looking at the offer, not at the bid. The offer was a free ticket for an activity that I might find mildly interesting but that would take a rare free evening. But the bid was, "Hey, let's connect on a deeper level. Let me introduce you to my family; let's find a time outside of work hours to connect."

I liked both these individuals. The invitations were rare. It wasn't the case that I had higher priorities or was short of time. I just didn't grasp the opportunities in front of me.

## The Work You Need to Do to Respond

Most of the work you do to attract a mentor or sponsor is simply the work you do every day. Mentors and sponsors are drawn to you because of how you are already showing up in the world. They notice potential and good character that are already being demonstrated. However, there are subtle things you can do to lasso them in. How can you notice the opportunity when it is there and not blow it?

### Notice and Name What You Are Noticing

Periodically, your path will cross with people who trigger a positive feeling in you. They seem cool, or they may ask you questions no one else does, or they may seem to have it all together. Maybe they understand you in a way slightly different from how other people understand you. Perhaps they seem successful and human.

## Develop Your Spidey Sense for Bids

Learn to examine the bids behind offers. "Let's go to a movie" means "Let's spend time together." "Let's brainstorm" means "I value your point of view." "Do you want to come with me and my wife to the opera?" means "I'd like to introduce you to my personal world."

People regularly ignore bids or let them drop, and this includes people who are eager networkers. For instance, I have delivered a lot of speeches and workshops over the past twenty years. I'm a good speaker and the topics are interesting to people, since they often deal with career angst and what to do about it, so typically a handful of people will come speak with me at the end. They ask for my card and frequently say, "I'd love to connect with you at some time."

I say, "Sure." But probably only 1 to 2 percent of people who come up to me ever make any further contact. They made a bid and I responded, but they aren't responding to the response.

## Make Space in Your Life for Mentors and Sponsors

Good mentors and sponsors are rare. If a potential mentor or sponsor makes a bid, respond positively. Don't make them stand in the same line as everyone else. Move your schedule. Go to an inconvenient part of town. Make some space for them.

Juan José García, who you met in the introduction, is a real person, and, as you have figured out by now, he is a real mentee. Since our initial connection in Washington and the time he drove three hours to Austin to meet me and my work friends, we have stayed in touch.

Our dinner in Austin was the first time I really got to know him. A week later, I started pinging him, "Did you follow up with those people? Don't wait." He had shown he was making space for this relationship, so I in turn began offering more. I began describing Juan and his job goals to people I met, and at one point I called up a partner I know in a major law firm to see if Juan could get an interview. That is moving into sponsor territory.

As you make more space in your life for these relationships, you feel more power to ask for what you want. A few months ago, Juan asked if I would write a recommendation for a prestigious Chambers Diversity & Inclusion: Future Leader award. I took a look at the criteria, and it was pretty heavy duty. They weren't asking for just a few vague lines of praise—it would take some real thinking. I'm a busy person, but I rolled up my sleeves and did it. Of course I did.

## Make Bids of Your Own

You can bid up. You can ask senior, powerful, accomplished people to further the relationship. You can:

- Invite them for coffee or a drink
- Invite them to events
- Send them fundraising appeals
- Keep them informed of your progress and explorations
- Send them articles of interest
- Introduce your family to them
- Invite them to visit you or stay with you
- Ask them to be your mentor

## TWENTY-MINUTES-A-DAY EXERCISES

- **Exercise 1:** Ask a friend or colleague if they have sponsors or mentors and how they came into their life.
- **Exercise 2:** Write a list of five people you could be a mentor to.
- **Exercise 3:** Read about how Valerie Jarrett met Barack Obama.

# CHAPTER 15
## Succeeding in Hierarchies

When I was twenty-four, I landed in what was then called Calcutta (now it's Kolkata) to start my first tour of my first real career. I arrived in India equipped with a black diplomatic passport, six weeks of full-time Bengali lessons, and great self-confidence along with great apprehension. Before leaving the U.S. for this big adventure, I had asked lots of experienced officers, both mid-level and more senior, for advice. Several of them were not shy about saying that the boss I was going to work under, Maurice, was not easy—he was described as a Cold War warrior who had served for many years in the East Bloc and was controlling and distrustful. I was told to watch myself around him.

When I met my new boss, his presentation didn't gainsay the gossip. He looked to me like a Cold War guy. He was forty years older than I was. He wore a safari suit to work every day, a garment favored by American diplomats in Africa and South Asia that features a jacket-shirt with big pockets and matching pants, usually in khaki or beige. We had weekly senior staff meetings, which included all the Americans, as well as the top fifteen

Indian staffers. We would sit in a circle in exact order of rank. First Maurice spoke, then the next most senior American, then the next, then me, then the most senior Indian, then the second most senior Indian, and so on. Once Maurice announced with a big toothy smile, "It looks like we're ready; the only thing that's not ready is my coffee!" At that, his executive secretary, a refined Indian woman in a sari, rushed in to serve his coffee. I heard the cup rattle against the saucer.

At that age, I thought of myself as a very sophisticated traveler but found the adjustment to Kolkata challenging. I spent a couple of months engaged in a type of ongoing confirmation bias, where I tallied the things I noticed that confirmed what I'd been told about my boss, while not actually looking for contradictory information. I thought of myself as a curious person, yet it didn't really occur to me to be curious about his own background and experiences. He was a little scary, and that was enough.

Then another problem gradually revealed itself: I couldn't seem to determine what my job actually was. Every day I read memos from the "Inbox," initialed them, and then put them in the "Outbox" (these were actual metal trays). I had a rotational position where I was supposed to generally learn the ropes, but I had no stated goals, no project teams, no KPIs. I attended gallery shows and parties and concerts but wasn't sure how it added up. I stared at the giant clock in my office, imagining my contemporaries starting law school and making progress on their fast-paced lives, while I sat bored and alone in my office, listening to the cawing of crows and the shouting of vendors in the rutted streets outside.

One day I wrote a note to my boss inviting him and his wife, Janet, to my apartment for Mexican food. I heard nothing. Then, at the end of meeting a few days later, he said, "Janet and I are looking forward to that Mexican food!"

My boss and his wife did indeed come over. Over ground beef tacos served inside Ortega taco shells shipped from the U.S., we chatted about this and that. He revealed that he knew I was dating the daughter of a Sikh general (I was hetero-curious). We talked about exercise (I said I that I practiced "calisthenics," concerned that admitting to "aerobics" wouldn't sound butch enough). And at one point he offered to serve as a father confessor if I ever needed advice. *Hard pass*, I would have said if that phrase had existed at the time. The whole time I felt I was putting on a performance, which I was, but it was a normal enough conversation.

Still, I felt different after that lunch. I didn't feel warmly toward Maurice, but I didn't feel intimidated either. While I didn't disbelieve the negative opinions that some people offered me, I started questioning whether they were the complete story and whether they were relevant for me. I had concluded by then that the Foreign Service was very gossipy. We didn't have streaming, cell phones, or even email, and we were constantly stressed out, so we entertained ourselves by talking.

Over the months that followed, I began figuring out how to create my own job, a skill that would prove valuable in the future. I got better at parsing the useful insights within the dramatic stories presented by others (such as: invite your boss to see the cultural events you put on so that he can see you in action and have material for your reviews). I plugged myself more into work, created projects I could execute, and made expat and Indian friends.

Maurice wasn't a mentor. He wasn't a boss who bent over backwards to set me up for success. But he wasn't my nemesis either. He didn't block me from action. He was just a person who had lived an entire lifetime before meeting me and whose style and opinions were shaped by another era; I likely wasn't his dream employee either. It took about five minutes of effort for me to invite Maurice and his wife over for tacos, but it served me better than all the negative energy I had invested in distrusting him.

Bosses are human beings. They have insecurities, areas of confidence, and ambitions. They have families, hopes, and losses. Most important for our analysis, they have needs. This is also true of everyone senior to you in any hierarchy.

Bosses have a great potential for helping you be successful. You can make them your asset. Your strategy from day one should be to understand them, help them meet their needs, and share what your own needs are. You don't need to scheme to do this. Just treat them by the same relationship code you would with anyone else.

Regarding bosses and senior stakeholders as beyond your zone of influence can be convenient for you because it lets you off the hook. But you always have options. You have choices about how to invest your energy. You have the power to create and leverage the relationships you need, even in hierarchical relationships.

## Redefining Power

People talk about power all the time: who has it, who doesn't have it, and how people without power are impeded from accomplishing anything. The question of "power" now shows up in workshops, mission statements, and strategic plans, and if you don't mention power when talking about personal progress, people think you are naive or just not getting with the program.

Power is relevant when it comes to career progress, but not in the way that academics and activists put it. Power exists, but it's not inherently a problem. It's just something to deal with.

Michael Wenderoth is an executive coach who has written an excellent book on power in the workplace, called *Get Promoted: What You're Really Missing at Work That's Holding You Back*. His view is that it's essential to understand how to use power but that it's not the evil, deterministic force that people who have taken Foucault seminars think.

Wenderoth first notes that "power is not coercion"[1] but rather the ability to get your way in the face of opposition. In the workplace, power does not come from identity categories, but instead from five specific *asset* categories:

1. **Political skills.** Your ability to navigate systems and cultures; your ability to manage personalities; your organizational intelligence.

---

1. Michael Wenderoth, *Get Promoted: What You're Really Missing at Work That's Holding You Back* (Unstoppable CEO Press, 2022), 19.

2.  **Strong networks.** Who you know, inside and outside the organiza-
    tion. Your ability to build, maintain, and leverage relationships.

3.  **Visibility and brand.** Visibility is the extent to which other stake-
    holders see what you are accomplishing. This could relate to the
    place your work has in the company's priorities or your skill in let-
    ting everyone know what you're doing. Brand refers to what you are
    known for—it's a combination of the value you deliver and your skill
    in communicating it.

4.  **Executive presence and communication skills.** Executive presence is
    the extent to which you command attention or are taken seriously.
    Whether people pay attention to you is partly defined by social
    biases (e.g., tall, slender man versus short, chubby woman) and
    partly defined by individual behaviors (e.g., crisp communication
    versus rambling on).

5.  **Control of hard resources.**[2] This refers to budget, hiring power, and
    specific authority within a job.

Only the last of these—control of hard resources—tends to relate to formal position. The rest are in the realm of soft power and are under your
control. If you don't have them, you can develop them.

## Hierarchies Are Normal

You have some relationships in your life in which you are on the same level
as the other person. Examples would be friends, some family members,
and work colleagues where you are at similar levels and don't report to each
other. This is also generally true of citizens in a democracy.

The U.S. as a culture places a strong value on equality. This means that
we want to behave in an egalitarian manner, and we want to *be perceived* as

---

2. Wenderoth, *Get Promoted*, 47.

egalitarian. Nearly ninety percent of Americans define ourselves as middle class, regardless of income, education level, or job.[3] Yet many of our relationships are hierarchical, and many relationships naturally have power differentials. Examples are:

- Boss/direct report
- Board/CEO or executive team member
- More experienced/less experienced
- Person with information/person seeking information
- Busy person/person seeking attention
- Person with formal authority/person without
- Insider/outsider

The power differential doesn't prevent any of these relationships. It's simply an aspect of the relationship.

The idea that power should *not* be part of relationships—that power is a problem that should go away as opposed to something you just deal with in life—is particularly American. In other countries hierarchical relationships are accepted and people deal with them. I can't think of another place where people feel they need to get rid of all power structures to move ahead. It's only in the richest country in the world with the most fluid class system that this belief is common.

## Decoding the Needs of Bosses

The most direct way to engage with a boss or other powerful person is to follow the "your needs, my needs" analysis. Ask yourself not just what your boss wants but what he or she actually needs.

---

3. Jeffrey B. Wenger and Melanie A. Zaber. "Most Americans Consider Themselves Middle Class, But Are They?" RAND Corporation, May 14, 2021, https://www.rand.org/blog/2021/05/most-americans-consider-themselves-middle-class-but.html.

I asked this of one of my clients, Jerome. He was a mid-level lawyer in a respected law firm. He was told that the firm respected his skills and intellect but that he needed to work on communications and "presence." Basically, he didn't make much of an impression. The partners wanted him to be clearer and more articulate, and to be someone whom clients would see as worth listening to. This wasn't as straightforward an instruction as you might think since it all had to be done within the boundaries of the firm's particular culture. Law firms are very hierarchical, and no one would mistake working at this white-shoe firm with spending a weekend at Burning Man.

A key place communications and "presence" seemed to come up was in conference calls with clients. The calls would be attended by Jerome, a senior partner, and a client.

I asked Jerome to mentally reenact one of these calls and to think of the partner's mental state. "What was the partner doing just before your call? What's going on in his head? How familiar is he with the matter? What does he want? What does he *not* want?" I asked.

As Jerome thought through these questions, it became clear that he was much more familiar with the deal than the partner. The partner had better overall judgment, but it was Jerome who was up to date on the details, the workplan, and any unresolved issues.

Jerome started coloring in the partner's mental state: he was probably busy until the last minute on something else, he was parachuting into this meeting for a short time, and after this meeting he would go to a meeting on a different deal.

What did the partner not want? The partner didn't want to sound out of the loop. Or unprepared. He wanted to deliver his wisdom efficiently, he wanted the client to be happy, he wanted to feel someone had his back.

Jerome had imagined the partner as the smart, authoritative boss. That's why Jerome had always taken his place at the back. He didn't want to step on any toes or impinge on the partner's authority. Jerome had never thought that a big scary partner might need someone to have *his* back. But he now realized that the partner depended on him more than he had imagined.

Now Jerome had insight into how *he* should show up. Instead of waiting for instructions from the partner, he created the agendas. Before the meeting, he sent an email to the partner identifying the top issues that might be discussed, summarizing them, and sketching out different options for dealing with them. At the start of each meeting, Jerome spent several minutes up front going over the recent history of the transaction so that the partner could silently ground himself. He played more of a facilitator role in the meeting so that the partner could pipe in when he wanted without feeling he had to run everything.

Everyone commented on how much more they were seeing from Jerome. "The client is really paying attention to you," the partner said, which meant the partner was paying attention as well. The secret to coming off as bigger was not being louder or more talkative; it was analyzing the partner's needs.

Don't treat your boss like a cardboard cut-out. Don't "otherize" them. Bosses are human beings with needs, just like everyone else.

## Exercise: Your Boss's Needs

Pick someone who you regard as a boss or senior stakeholder. Answer the following questions:

1. What do they need generally to be successful in their role?
2. What do they need from you?
3. Where are they in their own career? What are their hopes, fears, and so on?
4. What's something you have in common with them?
5. Which of your needs have you communicated to them?
6. Which of your needs have you *not* communicated to them?

## Factors to Manage in Hierarchical Relationships

Not all professional relationships are equal. When you are lower in the hierarchy, you will have to accommodate the other person. This doesn't make
you a serf. It just means you need to be clear about how some specific factors
affect your zone of action.

### Time

Assume that your boss, or any person more senior than you, is busier than
you are, at least in the work sphere. You have one boss, but he or she probably has multiple direct reports. Assume their time is scarce and that you are
going to comply with their schedule, not the other way around. Claim time
with them, just do so judiciously.

### Competing Concerns

Just because a decision doesn't go your way doesn't mean your boss is dumb
or hateful. A person managing and leading people has to be aware of and
make decisions about competing considerations. If I'm deciding who to staff
on an engagement, I will take into account the interests of the coach who
wants to do the gig, but I also evaluate what the client needs and the interests of other coaches. I will also assess my bandwidth for supervision.

### Knowledge Base

Your company believes that your boss has more experience and knowledge
in your industry. That's why he or she is the boss and not you. You might be
in charge with a specific area about which your boss knows very little, but he
or she will be more experienced overall. You can take issue with your boss,

but do so respectfully. Don't say, "I know a lot more than you." Say, "In this particular area, I have some special expertise I'd like to share."

## Respect

When you are dealing with someone senior to you in a hierarchy, you need to show respect for their knowledge, experience, position, time, and positive intentions. This doesn't mean being a doormat or silently acquiescing to everything. It does mean that you recognize that their achievements mean something, you understand what they have done to earn those achievements, and you respect how others view them.

I once had a conversation at a political fundraiser with a young gay guy who had worked on Capitol Hill and was considering business school. We had a pleasant, amusing chat for a few minutes. He eventually did go to business school and did the same program I did, a JD/MBA. There are very few people who have done this particular program, and maybe a handful of gay people who have done it, so it's a unique connection. Or so you might think.

A few years later, he reached to me to network. The subject line of his email to me was: "From one JD/MBA fag to another." I don't remember what specifically he asked me for, but I definitely remember the subject line.

I was taken aback. I wasn't offended or "harmed." I suppose in some environment I might boisterously refer to myself as a JD/MBA fag, though it wouldn't be my first choice of a witticism. What I found breathtaking was that this guy considered his email an effective way to network with me. Yes, I am an out, loud, and proud urban gay guy. Yes, I'm all for creatively reappropriating vilifying language. But I was also far more advanced in my career than he, we'd only met once years before, and he was looking for professional advice or connections. It wasn't offensive to me. It was overfamiliar.

I did not respond to his email.

## Compliance

When you're in a job, you're not part of the French Resistance. Hierarchical systems are not democracies. Not everyone has equal input. People above you make decisions, and your job is to carry them out. Opposing this or dragging your feet is insubordination. You cannot pick and choose what you will go along with in the workplace.

I'm regularly surprised by examples of people who are flat-out insubordinate at work: walking out of meetings, exiting video calls, or agreeing to something publicly and then working at cross-purposes behind the scenes. There's a role for vigorous debate and pushing others toward the right solution, but there's no such thing as "the loyal opposition" in a company or nonprofit organization. You're part of the same team, and if you aren't willing to execute on team goals, you need to be out of there.

## Scripts for Engaging with Bosses and Senior People

Open-ended questions are the most useful way to engage with bosses and other people who are senior to you or more powerful than you. Asking a question invites them to share, and open-ended questions stimulate creative thinking. An open-ended question cannot be answered with a "yes" or "no," and usually starts with "What," "How," or "Tell me more." Consider the difference in the two types of questions:

| Closed Questions | Open-Ended Questions |
| --- | --- |
| • Do you have any advice? | • What advice do you have? |
| • Did it take a long time to get up to speed in institutional sales? | • How did you get up to speed in institutional sales? |
| • Can you describe the most important factors in being an inclusive leader? | • What are the most important factors in being an inclusive leader? |

| Closed Questions | Open-Ended Questions |
| --- | --- |
| • Did you change as a result of working in China? | • How did you change as a result of working in China? |
| • Have you reached a decision? | • Where are you in your decision-making process? |

Asking great questions makes you sound intelligent and is generally safer than just presenting your own opinions. Here are some examples:

### Questions About Work Goals

1. "What are your own goals for this year? What would make you personally satisfied?"
2. "What do you like about being a manager? What's hard about it?"
3. "What do you know about this job that you didn't know when you started?"

### Personal Questions

1. "How long have you been at the company? I'd love to hear how you started out your career."
2. "How old are your children? What are their interests? Where do they go to school?"

### Feedback

1. "From your point of view, how did the meeting go?"
2. "What do you think we should do different next time, if anything?"
3. "I'd love to ask you for some feedback. What's going well, and what's an area I could improve?"
4. "I've been working on [name area: e.g., interrupting less or showing more presence] over the past few months. I'm curious what you've noticed."

**The Business**

1.  "From a business point of view, what do you see as our biggest priority?"
2.  "What's something on the horizon that we are going to pay more attention to in the coming years?"
3.  "What skills do you think we (or I) need to acquire to deal with this effectively?"
4.  "What's been the biggest surprise to you over the past few years?"

**Pushing Back on a Position or Idea**

1.  "I hear what you're saying. What I'm curious about is [name potential problem]."
2.  "I hear what you're saying. I know that Brenda has the same view. What I'm concerned about is [identify problem]."
3.  "I've been doing additional research on this particular question. Can I share what I've learned?"
4.  "Can I push back? I see what you're saying, but I've also noticed that [name issue]."

## Acknowledging a Screwup

You will screw up sometimes. It's inevitable. The important thing is how you handle it. A screwup doesn't have to damage a relationship. Sometimes it can improve it.

A few months into my new career as a corporate lawyer, I was working on a transaction with a South American natural resources company. I had been sent to South America to do due diligence, which amounted to spending many hours reading handwritten board minutes and making sure nothing was cause for concern.

We were closing the transaction, which included publishing a prospectus that would be filed with the SEC. This included being awake most of the night to make sure everything was happening on schedule and correctly.

The next morning, I was in the office and had one of those disconcerting realizations that I'd forgotten something—like a dream you're suddenly reminded of. Several days before, the main partner had asked me to review a short paragraph with the tax lawyer. I had forgotten to do this. No one else had spoken about it since then. *Was this maybe optional?* I asked myself, knowing the answer. It was practically the same transaction we did before, so maybe it didn't matter and the prior disclosure would be okay.

I knew I had blown it. I didn't know whether this was a real problem or just something that made me look unreliable. Either way, I knew I had to make the partner aware of it.

I went up and knocked on the door. "Um, Evan, I need to let you know . . ." I explained the problem. In live action before me, I saw his mind race as he spun through the different possibilities.

"I'll call Joanne," he said, referring to the tax lawyer. "Maybe we can sticker it." This mean we could print out stickers that would go over the printed part that was wrong, to avoid doing the whole thing over again. I was dismissed and went off to agonize in my office.

He called me later and said, "Good news, the tax disclosure is okay the way it is." I'd dodged a bullet. We had in fact done a similar deal before and the precedent language was still good. But this was no way to be a lawyer.

I went back to the partner's office. "Evan," I said, "I want to acknowledge that I screwed up. I didn't do something I should have, and I created a problem for you and the transaction. I'm sorry for this error in judgment, and I won't do it again."

At that point, a big smile broke out on his face.

"We all mess up, Michael," he said. "The important thing is just to learn from it. We're fine."

He smiled because I'd demonstrated I was someone he could deal with. I had self-awareness, which is what you most want and most often question in a younger employee.

If you screw up, follow this framework to acknowledge and move on:

1. Acknowledge what happened
2. Acknowledge impact
3. State your learning
4. State your intention to improve
5. Connect back to the relationship

## TWENTY-MINUTES-A-DAY EXERCISES

- **Exercise 1:** Complete the exercises in this chapter if you haven't done so already.
- **Exercise 2:** Use one of the suggestions in this chapter for pushing back. You can use this with a friend or colleague or try with a more senior person.
- **Exercise 3:** Pick three questions in the lists above to ask your boss at an appropriate time.

# CHAPTER 16
# Be a Benefactor

I started my coaching business during a historic recession. Many of my clients were unemployed and having a hard time of it. Others were employed and dissatisfied with their current positions but anxious about looking for something else. Recessions breed scarcity thinking—"There isn't enough to go around"—and for good reason.

My unemployed clients weren't losers. They'd studied hard, gone to good schools, and worked diligently to climb the ladder—but the game of musical chairs had stopped, and they were left without a seat. They were doing their best to improve their situations, but they also regularly felt regret, anxiety, and depression, along with a dose of "How did this happen to me?" They were trying to make opportunities materialize yet felt that little was under their control.

Amid these clouds, I noticed an interesting thing happening. My clients started reporting about advice *they* were giving to *other* job seekers, intermixed with expressions of their own turmoil.

"I still can't believe I'm in this position!" cried Helen, a lawyer. "How could I go from graduating honors at Penn Law School and clerking for a

distinguished judge to being rejected by third-tier firms in Connecticut?"
Then Helen mentioned as an aside, "The other day I was talking my cousin.
He just graduated from college and is looking, and his positioning statement
is terrible! He has a lot to offer but has no clue how to present himself. I
showed him the handouts and then rewrote his pitch for him and made him
practice in front of me a bunch of times until it was conversational. Now he's
fit for the workforce."

Or David might say, "I've had an interview with another management-
consulting firm, but I don't see how I can go back to the lifestyle. Beggars
can't be choosers, I guess." Then he'd change tone. "I caught up with a
neighbor from our kids' carpool. She's a teacher and wants to do something
new but hates the very idea of networking. She said, 'I'm an introvert and
I don't have enough contacts,' so I said, 'Let me set you straight on that.' I
explained 'the strength of weak ties' and drew the concentric circles diagram. It was a big aha for her."

Or Jung might say, "I've made it to three final-round interviews, but I
can't seem to clinch the job. There always seems to be an inside candidate,
and I feel like the search they are doing is just for show or to meet their EEO
requirements." Then she'd shift gears. "I told my mom about the Hudson
Cycle of Renewal you showed me and the idea of cocooning, the phase when
you're turning inward and sorting things out and you feel empty but you're
really getting ready for your next stage. She's been having a hard time since
my dad died. I told her there are times in life when it's okay to feel empty and
low energy. It's like winter when you're burrowed down and covered with
snow. Spring always comes. You'll eventually figure out who you are going
to be next. She seemed to get real comfort from that idea."

My clients were bummed about their own prospects. They didn't know
when good things would happen. Yet they retained the capacity to help others. They could teach lessons, share their connections, and be supportive,
even as they weren't entirely sure if the lessons would work for themselves.
Looking for jobs in a tight market, they were stymied in sharing their talents

and gifts with employers. But they were able to share valuable and unique things with other people in their lives.

The truth is you can always give. Thinking of yourself as a benefactor from day one shifts the whole energy of your career. And the more you give away, the more you have.

## Solving the Problem of Inexact Reciprocity

You can view the giving and receiving that are part of relationships as a series of specific transactions, or you can view them as a general flow. In this flow, you play both roles. You experience the back and forth. Today you may need to ask for something, tomorrow you may be able to offer something. If you believe that over time both of you are meeting your needs, you don't have to keep track of who's getting what in a specific exchange.

You can also think of your flow as being with the world as a whole, not simply with a set of discrete individuals. You *generally* give and you *generally* receive. It doesn't matter so much who you are giving to, just that you are giving. I help someone carry their suitcase up the subway stairs, and they make dinner for a housebound neighbor.

If I believe this theory, I don't need to worry about exact reciprocity as long as I work to achieve general human reciprocity. If a captain of industry makes an introduction for you to a potential business client, it's unlikely you will be able to do something similar for her. But you might make an introduction for someone in your own world that will make a difference.

I invest in flow more than specific transactions. I'm aware of specifics, and show appreciation for and remember them, but I don't try to match everything one for one. I go for the bigger equation. I advocate a loose rather than strict accounting.

I can't prove any of this, but I believe it. I like to think that the offering energy that Helen displayed in giving useful advice to her cousin balanced out the asking energy she needed to solicit connections to companies that would value her legal skills. And when David was explaining the strength of weak ties to his neighbor, he was making a deposit to the cosmic account that might also allow him to find a job that suited his personal values. And when Jung was sharing a new model for understanding life transition to comfort her mom, she was also opening herself up to get comfort from others.

If you accept these two, more expansive interpretations of how exchanges work—creating a flow rather than creating transactions and partnering with the world as a whole rather than a limited set of individuals—you have a lot more freedom of movement. You solve the problem of inexact reciprocity: the situation where what you want or need from someone else outweighs what you might offer them at that particular time—or perhaps ever. Your need is bigger, or more urgent, or more unusual. Sure, you're an engaging conversationalist and Rosalba might enjoy spending time with you, but Rosalba could put in a good word for you to the board. You could teach Dr. van der Schee how to make an excellent cilantro lime salad, which she might like, but if she agrees to speak to this year's medical graduates, you'll have an amazing ceremony.

If you generally commit to providing things of value to people— including people where you are getting little or nothing in return—it's okay for reciprocity to be inexact. Maybe reciprocity will come five years down the road. Maybe it will never come with this relationship, but in the bigger life and work equation, you'll balance it out with others.

A great way to anchor this equation in your life is to commit to be a benefactor. And I mean commit to this, right now, at whatever stage you are in your career and at whatever age. You don't need to wait, and you shouldn't. You can be a benefactor to the people in your invisible network, and the world at large, today.

## Ways to Be a Benefactor

Don't try to change lives. Just try to be useful.

A slogan I dislike is, "Be a volunteer and change someone's life." It's a bit sanctimonious and condescending. Sometimes you might have a huge impact on someone's life, but life is sufficiently complicated and unpredictable that I don't think you should make it your goal to go around trying to change people's lives. People can change their own lives. Being a benefactor doesn't mean being virtuous or being self-denying. It means finding ways to be useful and helpful to others.

You can help people at any juncture of your life, whether by providing advice, being a friend, giving money or information, or countless other ways.

Here are a few ways.

## Make Introductions

Relationships are wealth, and you can choose to give away wealth right now. The easiest way is by introducing people to each other. You are pointing out resources they might not know exist, and you are zeroing out any search cost for them.

A few years ago, I arranged for an au pair to live with our family and help take care of my sons. Paula was from a small city in Colombia, in her final year in college, and a go-getter. She was interested in having an international experience, and she picked my family.

When Paula arrived at our home in rural Western Massachusetts, she was very excited and also immediately homesick. At the au pair family orientation, I had seen a couple I recognized from my coworking space. They were hosting an au pair from Mexico, Zelda, who had already been in the area for several months. I asked for Zelda's info and sent her a text, explaining that Paula was new in town and I'm sure would benefit from a new friend.

Within an hour Paula had a date to meet Zelda and several other au pairs from Latin America and Europe. They met at a mall, went ice-skating, and had ice cream, and when Paula came back, she glowed. This connection was easy to make. It was zero cost and had a huge benefit.

Making introductions is powerful. The impact on others can be many times the effort it takes you. Make a habit of it. Don't worry about making the relationship happen—that's their job. You just need to light the match.

There are all kinds of bases for connecting people:

- Similar personalities
- Common situations
- Common interests
- New arrival in town or at a company
- In the same field
- Interest in learning about a different field
- Potential business contacts
- Potential mentor or protégé
- Services (e.g., doctors, personal trainers, mortgage brokers)
- Contact with a company or in an industry

Just ask yourself, "Who do I know who might benefit from meeting?"

## Share Useful Information

You can help other people by sharing useful information. This could include publicly available information like articles or TED Talks. It could also include specialty information, like recommendations on schools, summer camps, financial aid resources, leadership models, or amazing shows.

## Use Your Convening Power

You can create a group, host an event, or otherwise use your convening power. The world is filled with groups, clubs, associations, and networks, and in every one, people have worked hard to make it happen.

From the standpoint of the beneficiaries, it's wonderful to have someone who does this. I come to occasional meetings, meet new people, and hear new ideas, but I myself wouldn't organize most of them. I'm a cheerful and grateful free rider.

## Show Up and Be a Good Guest

Related to convening, you can help people out by joining *their* convenings.

Hosting parties can be fun but also stressful. If you go and show that you're having a good time, help people meet each other, and in general are a positive presence, you are doing the host a big favor. You can also show up early to help set up or stay late to help clean up. You won't be asked to do so, but unless they have a hired staff, your willingness will be appreciated.

## Be a Mentor

A mentor shares useful information or advice based on their own experience. You have helpful knowledge, and someone can benefit from it. You just need to offer it. Offering to be a mentor might seem presumptuous, or you may not think you know enough, or you may question the relevance of what you know. Like so much else, you figure things out by experimenting.

- "I can show you how to do that, if you like."
- "Would you like to hear my point of view?"
- "That happened to me when I was starting out here . . ."
- "I'm not naturally a good public speaker. But I wanted to become one. Would you like to hear how I did that?"
- "I'm a single parent as well. Once my sons turned five, it started getting easier. If you can survive until that point, you're all going to be fine."
- "Let's have lunch. I'd like to learn more about you and your goals."
- "I'm always happy to hear from you and get updates and answer any questions. Why don't you reach out every two months?"

There's uncertainty when you offer to be a mentor. Some potential mentees won't recognize what you are doing, and others say they want to move forward in their careers, but their actions say otherwise. That's okay. If someone doesn't see your value, that leaves a place for someone who will.

## Be a Sponsor

Sponsors make connections for people, create opportunities, and weigh in at crucial moments. They intervene in positive ways. If you have credibility and want to help someone who wants your help, you can be a sponsor.

A few years ago, a former colleague of mine, Mary, got a new position directing leadership development for a large nonprofit. She sent a message out to her network that she was looking for a number two—someone knowledgeable about coaching, leadership development, and organizational development, who was also good at getting things done. I thought of my friend, Anne, who had these competencies and more. Moreover, Anne was, by my analysis, stuck in a position that was beneath her capabilities. I could see both sides and *knew* that this would be an ideal match. I also felt that if Mary ever moved on to another position, Anne would be well situated to fill the top job.

I checked with Anne and told her I was going to recommend her. I gave Anne background information about the organization and offered my tips about how to engage with Mary. Then I called Mary and described Anne to her. I made no bones about it: "This is exactly the person you want. I know her very well, and I can guarantee she will be amazing. You don't need to interview anyone else."

Anne got the job. She was the exact complement to Mary, and she was overjoyed to get this particular job. It was a career breakthrough.

Facilitating a career breakthrough doesn't happen a lot—a handful of times in a twenty-year period. But it makes a great positive difference when it works.

## Support Others' Charitable or Political Causes

This is one of the easiest ways you can help people out and get their enduring appreciation. First, if someone has gone through the trouble of sending out fundraising invitations, they care a lot about the organization or candidate. Second, they are really hoping someone will respond. Asking people for money creates anxiety, and few people seem immune to this feeling. It almost seems that the more successful they are, the harder it is for them to ask, perhaps because they've always had the role of solving problems and saving the day rather than asking other people for help.

If you give something, even a small amount, it makes your friends happy, and they will remember it.

## Give Money and Resources

In my experience, it's empowering to give money away. The less money you have, the more powerful it feels to give to someone else. You're making a choice to establish yourself as a benefactor. It's as if you're telling the world, "Don't be fooled by my salary in the low five figures. I'm actually a generous and influential person in the world."

If you want to give away money, there are two ways to go: (1) just give some away or (2) reallocate your spending from something else. This can be small: give up one dinner out. Or make coffee at home for a week. Or stay in one night. Transfer what you would spend to the cause of your choice.

## TWENTY-MINUTES-A-DAY EXERCISES

- **Exercise 1:** Skip buying lunch or drinks for one day and redirect the money to something else.
- **Exercise 2:** Spend twenty minutes writing your manifesto about life and career success. Later, you can share your thoughts with someone on their way up.
- **Exercise 3:** Invite a younger person to lunch and ask them questions about their interests and ambitions.

# PART 5
# Keeping It Going

# CHAPTER 17
## How to Respond to Requests and Keep Boundaries

Early in my coaching career, I had a client I'll call Merrill. Merrill had a PhD in cultural anthropology but was working in public relations. She was unsatisfied in her job—she didn't have a lot of autonomy, and the firm was not managed well—and looking for something better. However, she felt her time and energy were being frittered away. For instance, at the request of a friend, she had taken a volunteer position on a board of a non-profit organization. She had to attend a lot of poorly run meetings and was asked to read piles of materials. To my ears, the other people on the board seemed both controlling and inept.

"Where is this going?" I asked.

"I don't know!" Merrill said.

"Why are you on this board?" I asked. "Do you care about the cause?"

"Because my friend said I should do it," she said. "And I do support the cause. And isn't it a good thing to be on boards?"

Well, I *guess*. Yes, it's good to give back, and being on boards can help you build your network, although they can also require a lot of work. I'm proud of my work on a nonprofit board and proud of the work the organization does. But it needs to be the right match.

Merrill was not someone who struck me as a pushover. She had what I call private sector energy. She was not a loud person but had a commanding presence. Her hair was jet black and she was put together in a very New York kind of way.

I had Merrill take the Myers-Briggs Personality Type Indicator, also known as the MBTI. She came out as ENTJ, a type sometimes called the Commander. In my MBTI certification training, we were specifically discouraged from typecasting people according to their results, but I threw caution to the wind. "Merrill, you need to be running something. You should be the boss. And you definitely need to get off this board. It's not a good use of your energy."

"I would love to run my own thing. Do you really think I can get off the board?"

"Just say, 'Thank for you this opportunity. I'm going in a different direction professionally, and I won't be able to fulfill the duties of the position.' Something like that. Don't overexplain it. It won't matter. No one is that essential. They will find someone else."

Merrill quit the board and quit her job and a few months later started her own consulting firm, which she's run successfully for more than fifteen years.

As you connect with your invisible network, you'll do a lot of asking. But relationships go both ways. You'll also *be asked* for things. Being a good person with thriving, healthy relationships doesn't mean you say yes to everything. If you do, your relationships aren't going to be thriving for long. If you can't say a real no, you can't say a real yes. When you commit your passion to one thing, you will have less of yourself available for another. To take on new goals, you may have to discard old ones.

The way you prepare for this is to understand your own needs, know where your boundaries are, and develop skill in responding to and negotiating requests. This includes using clean language so that you don't muddle your message out of a desire to seem nicer.

## Disappointing Others Is Inevitable, and Okay

Your choices and priorities will have an impact on other people, just as theirs will have an impact on you. This means that *inevitably* you will disappoint other people. Disappointing other people is not a great feeling, but in my view, it's better than feeling that you aren't living your own life, or the feeling of not being able to honor the commitments that are most important to you.

There are some other specific reasons why you have no choice but to set boundaries.

**Requests increase with success.** As you rise in your career, you will get more requests. You will have more resources to meet those requests, and other people will know it. You will also accumulate more connections simply through the accretion of jobs, moves, and experiences.

Some people get requests all the time, even early in their career. This is especially true if you are the "first"—the big success in your extended family, the one who has it all together. When you're in this position, you're perceived as both powerful and familiar. People perceive that you can do something for them, and they have less hesitation about accessing you. This is one reason why wealth accumulation is harder for people who come from low-income backgrounds—they may start playing the role of extended family philanthropist even in their twenties.

**Emotional fatigue.** Your time and resources are finite. Without some type of boundaries, at a certain point you are going to run out of time, energy, money, or compassion. You will get worn down, and helping people will no longer be pleasurable. Your own altruism deserves protection. You don't want to be in the situation where you shut down completely because of your inability to say no to unreasonable demands.

**Saying yes to the right things.** Some requests are better to accommodate than others. This is either because it is beneficial for you to say yes or because you are making a more unique contribution in some situations compared with others.

**Honoring your commitments.** Having integrity means you do what you say you will do, and you don't do what you say you won't do. To have integrity, you have to honor your commitments. This mean being realistic about what you can follow through on. It also requires you to be clear about what you are agreeing to.

## The Intersection of Capacity and Willingness

Whether you choose to help someone depends on two factors:

- Whether you in fact *can* help someone
- Whether you *want* to

I'll label these as capacity and willingness. Capacity depends on a combination of your skills and resources. Willingness depends on your own priorities as well as how you regard the person asking.

Consider the chart below:

|  | **Low Capacity** | **High Capacity** |
|---|---|---|
| **High Willingness** | You cannot help, but you would in different circumstances. | You are able to help, and you want to. |
| **Low Willingness** | You cannot help, and even if you could, you wouldn't want to. | You are able to help, but you don't want to. |

Only the upper right-hand quadrant shaded in light gray is where you should be giving to others. The dark gray quadrants are where people get in trouble—either by agreeing to things they can't actually deliver or by agreeing to things they don't really want to do.

## Negotiating Requests

As we discussed in chapter eleven, in response to any request, you can say yes, no, or make a counteroffer. Here are some examples:

**Request:** "I'm having a big party on a boat to celebrate my fortieth birthday. It'll be lots of fun, and it only costs $150 per person, including drinks."

> **(Yes)** "Sure, I'd love to come! Send me the deets."
>
> **(No)** "I won't make it, but thanks for inviting me. I hope you have a spectacular time."
>
> **(Counteroffer)** "Boats aren't my thing, but I'd love to take you out for breakfast at our favorite place the week after the party and hear all about it. How does that sound?"

**Request:** "I'm putting together a K-pop dance class for the first graders. I've lined up a great teacher, and we can do it in a studio near the school. I need six kids and have four right now. Can Ricky join us?"

> **(Yes)** "I've been looking for a dance class for him, and I'm sure he'd love it. We're in!"
>
> **(No)** "That's kind of you to invite him. We're going to pass."
>
> **(Counteroffer)** "This won't work for his schedule, but maybe we can set up a playdate soon. He's always talking about how much fun he has trading Pokémon cards with Nico and Mateo."

**Request:** "Since Katy's departure, I've taken on some of her responsibilities as well. I'd like my salary to reflect my value, hence I'd like a raise."

> **(Yes)** "You're right. Starting March, we can bump you up by 5 percent. At the end of the year, we'll do the annual comp survey and assess where we are."
>
> **(No)** "You are valued, and I've seen you pitching in more after Katy left. We only do raises on an annual basis when we do our annual comp survey."

**(Counteroffer)** "I've observed your dedication. We can't do raises in a one-off way, but let's talk about additional ways I can support your growth. I'm speaking to Bernard this afternoon, and I'm going to mention how much you've been doing since Katy left. There might be a way to shift some of your old responsibilities to other team members. How does that sound?"

Negotiation is important when people make requests of you because their initial request of you is often what they *think* they want or possibly what they think *you* want.

Here's an example. Let's say you're speaking to a classmate who has a start-up. Within forty-five minutes, she offers you a job. It's flattering and there could be a big upside, but you know the risks of start-ups, and you're not really sure what you want to do next. If you have *some* interest, you can start much smaller. You could be an advisor. You could do a short-term consulting project. You could offer to help them find other worthwhile candidates. You could be a friend who helps them forget about work.

You can help people by changing their conceptions of what they need. For instance, I'm on the nominations committee of a nonprofit board. For several years, we've had the idea that we needed to get some tech people on the board, since part of our mission is to help young people with career planning and tech is a part of so many careers. I set up a conversation with a former client of mine who's worked at several notable tech companies and currently manages hundreds of engineers. Could he help us find a new board member?

Steven went straight to the point: "Engineers don't want to go to boring meetings. They like to work on projects. They're not going to be happy going to meetings with a bunch of lawyers and bankers. On the other hand, engineers would be interested in doing some type of project with kids, like a hackathon. They love making things, and they love sharing their passion for the work. If you set that up, I know a lot who would love to participate."

A hackathon! Such thoughts had never entered our lawyer-banker minds, but we were instantly intrigued. We realized that we had been on the wrong track in terms of trying to nab a tech person to be on the board. Within six months of this conversation, we had forged a partnership with developers for a well-known video game company whereby developers would teach students in the school's games club how to build video games, and in the process offer insight into getting into a tech career without needing to earn a university degree.

## Use Clean Language

You need to be able to deliver a clean no. Muddling your language with misdirection and mixed messages doesn't help you or the relationship.

Here are some ways we muddle our noes.

### Can't Versus Won't

A common crutch is to say you can't do something rather than you won't or don't want to:

- "I can't discount my rate."
- "I can't dip into my savings."
- "I can't ask my family to move to another city."

You're saying, "I'm not deciding against this. I am just prevented by other forces from doing this." The truth is that you could do this, you just don't want the consequences of doing so.

The trouble is that when you say you have no agency, you start to believe it. Further, both of you understand on some level that you are not telling the truth.

### Overstating Enthusiasm or Regret

You're not going to do something but rather than leaving it at that, you overemphasize how wonderful the thing would be. "OMG, I would love, love, love to do that, but I can't that weekend."

## Excessive Detail About Your Decision-Making Process

This tends to come in the work realm, when you're denying a request for a raise, a new position, and so on. It's useful to say you've given something serious consideration, but you don't need to give a mind-numbing explanation of why. The other person will still be bummed, and all your verbiage won't make them feel less so.

## Muddling Negative Feedback

Sometimes you need to deliver a clear message that someone's performance has been inadequate, that they've made errors, or that their behavior needs to change.

People can find it difficult to take negative feedback. But muddling the message with qualifiers, false assurances, and extra words doesn't make the other person feel better. It makes them feel worse, because they know that something real is lurking beneath your words.

If it's your responsibility to deliver feedback to someone, the best thing you can do for them is to be clear about it.

# Additional Tips for Maintaining Boundaries Under Pressure

## Don't Say Yes on the Phone

Don't say yes on the phone[1] or when under pressure.

Memorize the phrase, "I'll think about it and get back to you."

---

1. Gretchen Rubin credits her father for this excellent advice.

## Practice Active Listening

Active listening is repeating back what the person is saying and checking for understanding. This slows you down in emotionally fraught circumstances and also makes the other person feel heard.

"So let me summarize what you just said. You have an upcoming interview and you want to know if I can recommend you personally. Is that right?"

Then, either, "I understand how that would be valuable, but it's not something I will do," or "I'm going to reflect on that."

## Make Beneficiaries Compete with Each Other

Instead of evaluating each request as it comes in, decide ahead of time how much you want to give, whether it's time, money, mentorship, connection-making, and so on. Compare all of the requests together, and decide which of those you want to respond to.

I give this advice to newer coaches who often feel anxious about charging people for their work. They sincerely want to help people and they know that many people struggle economically. They can easily find reasons why they should lower their rates or work for free.

My view is that it's great to do pro bono or low bono work, but decide how many slots you are going to put in this category, and then decide who merits those slots.

Other forms of this are:

- Set an annual budget for charitable donations.
- Decide how many people you are going to mentor at once.
- Set up "office hours" where you are open to anyone hitting you up for a conversation or advice.
- Decide how frequently you are going to make introductions.
- Decide on a profile of the kind of person you want to help.

## TWENTY-MINUTES-A-DAY EXERCISES

- **Exercise 1:** Negotiate your next invitation. Suggest a change to the format, location, or time. This is to help you practice meeting your needs in a low-stakes environment.

- **Exercise 2:** Fill out this sentence five different ways: "Because I'm going to say yes to _____, I'm going to say no to _____." (Example: "Because I'm going to say yes to getting through tax season in a healthy manner, I'm going to say no to drinks with friends until the end of March.")

- **Exercise 3:** The next time you have to say no by email or give some difficult feedback, ask a friend or colleague to review it to see if your language is clean and clear.

# CONCLUSION

# One Hundred Twenty-Minutes-a-Day Activities by Category

There you have it. You know how to create, maintain, and leverage relationships and develop the full potential of your invisible network. Having gotten to this conclusion chapter, you are doing the work already. You're underway.

One of the points of this book is that progress comes in regular, small steps rather than through grand gestures. So long as you keep things going, you will make big progress over time.

To help you chug away, here are a hundred additional Twenty-Minutes-a-Day activities arranged by topic. Do them in any order, checking them off as you go. Many of these would be good to repeat multiple times.

I can't wait to see where you end up.

**Building Your Network**

1. Search your laptop for the past several reaching-out messages you've sent and put them in the "drafts" folder, so that you can draw on them in the future.

2. Go on LinkedIn. Spend time liking, commenting on, and/or forwarding posts. People always notice who is commenting on their posts.

3. Go on LinkedIn. Spend time looking up people from past jobs and see what they are up to now. If you discover they are doing something new, write a quick note of congratulations.

4. Go on LinkedIn. Click on "My Network" and examine the "People You May Know" tab. Send some connection requests.

5. Reach out to someone with a different tool: if you normally text, make a call; if you call, send them a message on Slack; if you meet for drinks, suggest that you meet for breakfast.

6. Work with the deliberate social contagion idea. On a blank page, draw the radar screen. Think about a specific world you'd like to be more involved in—creatives, politicos, entrepreneurs, sports, spiritual people—whatever draws you. Fill in the diagram for just those people.

7. Have a call or set up an activity with one of those people from the prior exercise.

8. Ask people for recommendations about podcasts that relate to this area of interest. Facebook is a good platform for this kind of request.

9. Spend twenty minutes sampling one or more of the podcasts. For a couple of weeks, restrict your podcast listening to this area—nothing else. The idea is to surround yourself with voices and invite this social contagion to affect you.

10. Introduce two contacts who have the same interests—basketball or Korean food or start-ups, anything.

11. Introduce two contacts who are in the same career but who don't know each other.

12. Introduce two contacts who are dealing with the same thing.

13. Introduce two contacts who are from different generations. Explain why you think they should meet each other.

14. Make a list of five people in your industry whom you would like to meet in the coming year. If you're not sure who you should meet,

write to two friends or colleagues, and say, "For my professional development, I want to challenge myself to meet five key people in my industry over the next year. Who should be on my list?"

15. Spend twenty minutes looking at public information about one of the people on your list. You can look at LinkedIn, company websites, personal websites, Twitter. Repeat with others.

16. If you are expected to do fundraising for an organization, go through your calendar for the past year. Write down the names of new people you've met who you can list as prospects.

## Maintaining and Deepening Relationships

17. Call your mom or dad. If they aren't living, call another older person. Let them talk about whatever they want to talk about. Try not to be the one to hang up.

18. Share an unresolved issue with someone. Tell them you're not looking for a solution, you just want to share something on your mind.

19. The next time you are stuck in a boring place (such as in an airport or waiting in the school pick-up line), challenge yourself to send a bunch of friendly texts to weak ties—not the usual suspects, but people you aren't regularly in touch with. See how much value you can get out of this dead time.

20. Do a twenty-minute walk-and-talk with a contact. You can do this together or chat by phone.

21. Craft your version of a perfect (or at least acceptable) *no response required* email or text. This is the "Hey, I was thinking of you" or "Read this article and thought you might like it" kind of message. Challenge yourself to use this several times this week.

22. Create a set of soft but interesting interview questions for people you work with. These could include: (1) What do you like about your job? (2) What's the hardest thing about it? (3) What makes your day? (4) What demotivates you? (5) What are you looking forward to in the next year? Make your own list.

23.  Use these questions the next time you have a meeting with a colleague or direct report. You can just ask them, or you can say, "I just read a book on relationships, and it suggested some questions I ask my colleagues. Can I try them on you?" Give your own answers if they are interested. Repeat.

24.  Suggest to your boss or team that you use these questions as an icebreaker at your next meeting. If people take a moment to jot down their thoughts, they can answer all the questions in ninety seconds. Say, "A book I just read by an executive coach suggested this as an icebreaker."

25.  Go to a card store, drugstore, or large supermarket, and stock up on birthday cards. You can keep these as a backup supply (for instance, for work colleagues), or you can plan to send them out to specific people when birthdays roll around.

26.  Go to a card store, drugstore, or large supermarket, and buy a bunch of cards for an upcoming minor holiday (St. Patrick's Day, Halloween, Thanksgiving, etc.). These are sold months in advance.

27.  Send out your minor-holiday cards. You can do this whimsically or seriously, whatever your style.

28.  For people forty-plus: Write down a short professional chronology of key steps—college, first job, second job, etc. Next to each, write down the name of someone you spent a lot of time with or felt a close connection to at the time.

29.  Reach out to several of those people. Say, "I'm taking the time to look back at some of the key moments in my life and some of the important people, and I thought of you. I'd love to catch up. I am curious what you remember about me from that time."

30.  Have conversations of twenty minutes or more with each of those people.

31. If you are not religious or are mildly religious, talk to a religiously observant person about what their faith adds to their life. The purpose is listening, not debating.

32. If you are religiously observant, talk to someone from another religion about what faith adds to their life. The purpose is listening, not comparing.

33. Send a *Hang in there* message to someone. This is an encouraging note to someone who is dealing with a challenge. "I was thinking of you and your kids being stuck in your apartment with COVID for ten days, and I just want to send along some good thoughts. Hang in there."

34. Send a *You can do it!* message to someone. For instance, maybe they are trying to finish a manuscript. "Keep writing! This is the home stretch. I know you can do it!"

35. Send a *This sucks; I'm on your side* message to someone. "I'm sorry your ex is being such a jerk in the custody proceedings. This sucks; I'm on your side." "I'm sorry the insurance company is battling your flood claim. This sucks; I'm on your side."

## Self-Awareness

36. Write three big questions you're trying to answer in your life.

37. Complete this sentence five to ten times: "This year, I'm interested in learning more about . . ." Drop some of these statements into your conversations in the next weeks.

38. Make a list of your A people—these are people who give you energy. Write down the top three names and put them on a Post-it note. Put it on your computer or in your wallet.

39. Read about Gary Chapman's *The Five Love Languages.* Ask a friend, relative, or colleague what their love languages are.

40. Take the Enneagram personality assessment. The Enneagram types represent nine different strategies for dealing with life and have a lot to say about how we manage relationships. There are plenty of free versions online, or you can pay around $12 and take a more official one at EnneagramInstitute.com.

41. Take a personality test based on Jungian archetypes. These relate to differences in how we get energy, take in information, make decisions, and organize our lives, and therefore have a lot of insight about how we relate to others. This is the theory that supports the more widely known Myers-Briggs Personality Type Indicator. You can easily find a free version, which will be called something different from this, like "16 Personalities" or "Jungian Archetypes." You can take the official MBTI online for around $50 by going to www .mbtionline.com.

42. Take Gretchen Rubin's Four Tendencies personality quiz. The Four Tendencies explain differences in approaching habits and commitments. You can take this at www.quiz.gretchenrubin.com.

43. Take the DiSC personality test. The four DiSC variables are dominance, influence, steadiness, and compliance, and offer a lot of insight into how we and others show up at work. You can easily find a free version on the web.

44. Take the Big Five personality test. The Big Five traits are extroversion (also often spelled extraversion), agreeableness, openness, conscientiousness, and neuroticism. The Big Five is the one personality test clearly backed by psychological research. (That said, I find the not-scientifically-backed Enneagram more useful.)

45. Prepare for a mini-360 of yourself. Create a list of questions such as:
    - What's something I do well?
    - What's another thing I do well?
    - What's something I could improve?
    - What's a talent or characteristic I could lean into more?
    - Where do you see me in five years?

Reach out to several people whose judgment you value, and say you'd like to ask them these questions.

46. Conduct one of the 360 interviews. Ask them these questions. Don't overexplain. Just ask the question, keep your mouth shut, and write down their answer. Conduct another one of the 360 interviews. Repeat several times.

47. To focus more on the real world rather than the virtual world, change settings on your phone to grayscale for a few days. Your phone retains its functionality, you just will find it much less enjoyable and will spend less time on it. See this article in *Wired*: https://www.wired.com/story/grayscale-ios-android-smartphone-addiction/.

48. Have lunch alone, without your phone. Be willing to be bored.

49. The next time you drive for twenty minutes or more, put your phone in your trunk and keep the radio off.

50. If you go from busy work to busy homelife, try pulling over a mile before you get home. Be still and quiet for ten to fifteen minutes, then resume your journey home.

51. If you have kids or pets, watch them do something for twenty minutes without any kind of distraction. Just watch them participating in life for twenty minutes.

## Learning and Sharing

52. Read "How to Stay Stuck in the Wrong Career," by Herminia Ibarra, which you can find at https://hbr.org/2002/12/how-to-stay-stuck-in-the-wrong-career.

53. Send Herminia Ibarra's article to three mid-career friends who have mentioned career frustrations. Say, "This article really sparked my thinking. You might find it interesting."

54. Watch Susan Cain's nineteen-minute TED Talk, "The Power of Introverts," which you can find on YouTube.

55. Send Susan Cain's TED Talk to three friends. Say either, "As an introvert, this really resonated, and I thought you might like it," or

"As an extrovert, I learned a lot from this talk about how introverts experience the world, and I thought you might like it."

56. Download Jessica Pan's funny and moving book, *Sorry I'm Late, I Didn't Want to Come*, about the experience of an introvert trying to be an extrovert for a year, and read it in twenty-minute chunks.

57. Read John Kotter's article, "What Leaders Really Do," which you can find at https://hbr.org/2001/12/what-leaders-really-do.

58. Send Kotter's article to someone in a leadership role, saying, "Here's an interesting point of view about the difference between management and leadership. It really made me think."

59. Read reviews for *Managing to Change the World: The Nonprofit Manager's Guide to Getting Results* by Alison Green and Jerry Hauser. A client who has worked in multiple levels of government and in nonprofits told me this is by far the most useful book she's read on the subject.

60. Send a copy of *Managing to Change the World* to someone you know who works in the nonprofit sector and send another copy to an idealistic recent college grad.

61. Order a copy of the Next Step Partners' *Career Handbook for Working Professionals* (which I contributed to). You can get this on Amazon. Order another copy for a contact who is thinking about or engaged in a career transition.

62. Spend twenty minutes paging through the *Career Handbook for Working Professionals*. Make notes for the exercises that would benefit you. Keep this workbook nearby so you can dip into it each time you have ten to twenty minutes free.

## Mentors and Sponsors

63. Write a "job description" for a potential mentor.

64. Ask a friend or colleague if they have sponsors or mentors and how they came into their life.

65. Send an article or a video link of interest to a potential sponsor/mentor.

66. Ask a senior person who their sponsors or mentors have been.

67. Write a list of five people you could be a mentor to.

## Gratitude and Appreciation

68. Write a thank-you email or note for a social event. It could have happened recently or a few weeks ago. Say it was wonderful to spend time together and you appreciate being invited/their attendance.

69. Write a thank-you email or note to a colleague who has done right by you in the past weeks or months. Acknowledge their effort and/ or skill and describe the positive impact it had on you.

70. Write a thank-you email or note to a past boss, teacher, or mentor. Describe the ways they set a good example for you and/or the difference they made in your work or life. If they gave you specific advice that you remember, remind them of that.

71. Write a thank-you email or note to someone who helped you out in your personal life—childcare, a move, sympathy at a hard time, and so on.

72. Write a thank-you email or note for something for which you should have said thank you a *long* time ago—a gift, an act of service, words of wisdom. Say, "Many months (or years) ago, you helped me by _____. I didn't thank you at the time, even though what you did meant something important to me. I'm thanking you now. It did mean a lot."

73. Go to Goodreads or Amazon and read reviews of the book *The Thank-You Project* by Nancy Davis Kho. If it speaks to you, read it.

## Apologies

74. Apologize for a work screwup. "I made a mistake, I understand the impact it had, and I will do better next time."

75. Apologize for a faux pas. "I said this, or did this, it was dumb, and I'm sorry."

76. Offer someone an "I was not at my best" message. "I just wanted to let you know that I was not at my best at the meeting/dinner/party. I'm sorry."

77. Offer someone a "You were right, and I was wrong" message. "For a long time, I insisted that I knew how to manage money and I disputed you when you said that I was a spendthrift and would regret it one day. But now I realize that you were right, and I was wrong."

## Attending Events

78. If you haven't already, install Venmo or another payment app on your phone. The next time you are out socializing and someone else pays, Venmo them your contribution. They might return it but will probably appreciate the courtesy. Young professionals do this as a matter of course, but older people (like me) may not be familiar with this until they see it in action.

79. Find an event you might be interested in. Write to a cheerful friend. "I'd like to get out more. I want to go to this event. Will you come with me?"

80. The next time you attend a party, decide your job is to be consistently helpful to the host or hostess—to help them have a great event. Your attendance is merely a ruse for this secret mission.

81. Before your next party or professional gathering, make a specific plan about: (1) what time you will arrive and leave; (2) how many people you will talk to; (3) what you will eat (and not eat) and what you will drink (and not drink).

82. In preparation for your next group event, invent an alter ego. I once had a character called "Eli the Israeli Tourist." Things that bother Michael (like smoking or loud people) don't bother Eli—he's chill.

83. Make a budget for lost registration fees. The idea is to encourage you to sign up without feeling locked in or too worried about scheduling.

84. Sign up for an event or conference; pay the registration fee, even if you don't go.

85. Research the speaker for an upcoming event. Write down three questions you'd like to ask them. Don't worry about whether you ask the questions. They'll probably show up in your conversations with other people.

86. Find out the name of the person at your college or graduate school who puts on alumni events. Introduce yourself and say you'd love to attend any upcoming events in your area. "What do you have in the works?" You can also ask about virtual events. It's very easy to call people in these roles. They are eager to provide something useful to alumni and are interested in your feedback and ideas. Try this even if the school sends emails informing you about upcoming events.

## Convening

87. Initiate a group text or email to a set of friends you like but don't see together. "Hey, let's all get together in person. Let's talk location and dates."

88. Host a potluck (or carryout) dinner. "This is low-key, easy, and fun, and we can do it at my place."

89. Identify an alpha—someone who seems socially energetic and/or good at getting things going. Propose an activity to this person—"It would be great if we could get all the dads together for a beer night," or "It would be great if all we have a night out for LGBT staff and friends." Say something like, "I have some ideas, but you're so great at planning things."

90. The next time you assemble a group of people, whether for a party or a meeting, start with a specific icebreaker. "Let's start by sharing your name, where you work, and your favorite character on *Succession*. I'll go first." "Let's start by sharing your name, where you grew up, and a special talent or interest you had as a kid. I'll go first." People want to connect but often feel inhibited. If you give them something specific, it's easier for everyone.

91. If you are a member of a professional association, spend twenty minutes researching your peers. Look at the membership list. Look up some bios. Assess what you have in common with others and what impresses you about them.

92. The next time you go to a professional conference, plan a small personal event. Reach out to several people and ask them to meet for a drink, breakfast, coffee, and so on.

93. The next time you visit another city where you know people, try sending out a group message or even posting on Facebook, "Hey, I'm in town and would love to see everyone. I'll be at El Rey on U Street from 6:30–9:00 PM." See what happens. I tried this and it worked! Someone I hadn't seen in twenty-five years showed up, plus a lot of recent acquaintances.

94. Spend time contemplating an event that is beyond your normal convening. It might be a sit-down dinner for eight, a big house party, a pub crawl, a group trip to a concert, a hike up a mountain with friends. Something that is a stretch and a little scary. Sketch out your ideas for twenty minutes.

95. Book the date of this big event. Give advance notice to two to three guests. Ask them for further suggestions.

96. At the end of your next meeting, spend five to ten minutes taking stock of what has been accomplished. Questions you could ask: "How effective has this meeting been for us?" "What has been the best part of this meeting?" "What would we do differently next time?"

## Being a Benefactor

97. Make a budget for charitable donations for the next year. Create a total amount and decide how many different donations you want that to represent. Make a vow to give exactly that amount, no more and no less.

98.  Make a list of ways you can potentially help others. Think (1) skills, (2) connections, (3) caring, and (4) resources. Jot down what you can potentially do under each category.

99.  Invite a recent grad or young person to lunch. Alternately, reach out to the parent of a recent grad or young person and offer to talk to their kid about careers and networking.

100. Spend twenty minutes writing down your Career Manifesto—your affirmative rules for a fulfilling and successful career. The rules should be prescriptive—"do this" and "don't do that."

# ACKNOWLEDGMENTS

A major reason this book is an actual published thing and not something I would just carry around in my head for a decade is that I met Jennie Nash, my book coach. I appreciate Jennie's intelligence, energy, and directness: in reaction to an earlier, different proposal, she said, "I don't believe you really want to write this book. What book do you actually want to write?" The book I actually wanted to write was this one.

My gratitude to my clients, old friends, and new connections who allowed me to share their stories. Thank you to Juan José García, Halley Li, TaTy'Terria Gary, Soledad Roybal, Henry Robles, Desiree Portillo-Rabinov, Harrison Ross, Niki Khoshzamir, and Meghan Daum. Thank you to the real people behind the fictional names Mihai Ionescu, Anjali Sinha, Veronica, Rishi, and Merrill. Thank you to Caitlin, Ana, Barrett, Leticia, Faith, and Colin. Thank you to everyone else whose stories and experiences contributed to this book.

My mom, Trini Urtuzuástegui Melcher, has given me useful career advice (including the gem that you should network with people older than you), and I'm proud that sometimes I even listened to it.

Before he became my literary attorney, Tim Brandhorst was my editor at ABA Books. Thank you for seeing something special in *The Creative Lawyer* and for regularly asking me when my next special thing would come along.

The BenBella team has inspired me with their kindness and high standards. Matt Holt made me feel welcome and valued from the get-go. To Gregory Newton Brown, my very own personal editor: thank you for disregarding my instruction to get out your red pen and let it rip and instead telling me everything you liked about my draft and what you wanted to see more of. Alyn Wallace, I learned a lot about writing from your deft copy editing. Thank you to senior editor Katie Dickman for shepherding everything through. Brigid Pearson, thank you for the patience you showed in the cover design process, as well as for your beautiful workmanship. Thank you to Jessica Rieck for the design of the book interior—who knew fonts and tables could look so good? Thanks also to Kerri Stebbins and Mallory Hyde for marketing guidance.

My partners in MGM, Marci Alboher and Gretchen Rubin, have been the best kind of grown-up friends: supportive, enthusiastic, and not above saying, "You just need to write this." I love our special club, and I thank those earlier versions of ourselves that decided we should make plans to meet regularly.

Writing this book has been a good, if intense, way for me to examine what is really important to me since there are times when I would ask, "What is the point of this? What is the point of *anything*?" Well, that's easy for me. For me, the point of everything is Nico and Mateo, my sons. I won the lottery twice when I became a dad to you. Parenting isn't for everyone, but it was the best thing to ever happen to me. Thank you to Caitlin and Jillian for helping me to have this life.

# INDEX

# ABOUT THE AUTHOR

Michael Urtuzuástegui Melcher is one of America's leading executive coaches and is an expert on leadership and career development.

Michael's clients have included leaders in law, media, finance, private equity, consulting, technology, global health, foundations, environmental advocacy, and government. He has delivered coaching and leadership programs across the United States and in a dozen countries in Europe, Latin America, Asia, and Africa.

He previously held positions in a venture-backed start-up, as a lawyer with the firm Davis Polk & Wardwell, and in the U.S. Foreign Service, where he was posted to India and Taiwan.

*Your Invisible Network* is his third book. Michael is also the author of *The Creative Lawyer*, a self-coaching book for lawyers, and was the coauthor along with three college classmates of *The Student Body*, a novel about a prostitution ring at Harvard that was published under the pen name Jane Harvard. He has published numerous articles and has been quoted in the *Wall Street Journal*, the *New York Times*, and *Fortune*. He has hosted two podcasts.

Michael was born in Kent, Ohio, and grew up in Arizona and Southern California. He attended public schools and was the first student in his high school's fifty-year history to attend Harvard, where he earned a BA in government. He later earned a JD/MBA from Stanford. His mother, who raised him and his sisters as a single parent, was the first Hispanic woman in the U.S. to earn a doctorate in accounting.

He lives with his twin sons in Manhattan.